D0502607

— YOUNG READERS' EDITION —

THREE DAYS
— AT THE —
BRINK

FDR'S DARING GAMBLE
TO WIN WORLD WAR II

ALSO BY BRET BAIER WITH CATHERINE WHITNEY

Three Days in Moscow:
Ronald Reagan and the Fall of the Soviet Empire

Three Days in January:
Dwight Eisenhower's Final Mission

— YOUNG READERS' EDITION —

THREE DAYS
— AT THE —
BRINK

FDR'S DARING GAMBLE
TO WIN WORLD WAR II

BRET BAIER

WITH CATHERINE WHITNEY

HARPER

An Imprint of HarperCollinsPublishers

Library of Congress Catalog Number: 2019947144
ISBN 978-0-06-291537-5

Typography by Catherine San Juan
19 20 21 22 23   PC/LSCH   10 9 8 7 6 5 4 3 2 1

First Edition

*To the veterans of World War II and D-Day who died
on the beaches of Normandy and to those who are still living today.
Thank you for your service, sacrifice, and for saving the world.*

— CONTENTS —

INTRODUCTION: FINDING FDR   ix

PROLOGUE: THE "BIG THREE" DINNER PARTY   xiii

PART ONE: THE MAKING OF FDR

1   TO WHOM MUCH IS GIVEN   1

2   INTO THE ARENA   13

3   POLIO   27

4   IN THE FOOTSTEPS OF COUSIN TEDDY   40

PART TWO: SEEKING GREATNESS

5   PRESIDENT ROOSEVELT   53

6   GOVERNING IN CRISIS   61

7   FRANKLIN AND WINSTON   73

8   THE RISE OF THE ALLIES   88

9   THE COMMON CAUSE   95

PART THREE: THREE DAYS AT THE BRINK

10 THE ROAD TO TEHRAN   119

11 YOUR HOUSE IS MY HOUSE   135

12 CLASH OF TITANS   145

13 LIKE A RAINBOW   152

PART FOUR: THE ENDGAME

14	**AT LAST, OVERLORD**	165
15	**FDR'S FINAL ACT**	177
16	**THE WORLD HE LEFT BEHIND**	194
	ACKNOWLEDGMENTS	208
	GLOSSARY	211
	SOURCE NOTES	213
	INDEX	233

— INTRODUCTION: FINDING FDR —

The past is ever present. As the United States and the world paused to commemorate the seventy-fifth anniversary of D-Day—the most important battle of World War II—I was completing my work on this book. As the leaders of the free world stood on the cliffs above the Normandy beaches where they were once united in common cause, I reflected on all that brought them to that point.

I wrote this book because I wanted to capture that moment of time. It was during the three critical days of the Tehran Conference where the decision was made to launch Operation Overlord, the battle that came to be known as D-Day. World War II still has an influence on our lives, although it is growing more distant. The Department of Veterans Affairs reports that those who served in that war are dying at a rate of 372 veterans per day. Sixteen million of them fought; only 600,000 remain. How do we preserve the experience of that time and explain its meaning for the present and for future generations? I always tell my two sons, Paul, age twelve, and Daniel, age nine, that history is a living thing, and

I've found that to be true for myself. I was born twenty-six years after D-Day, but growing up I felt as if it was part of my story too. Respecting and revering the veterans who came to be known as the "Greatest Generation" was standard practice. Today, as the remaining veterans of D-Day live out their final years, we can see in their faces our greatest legacy as a nation.

Writing about history involves visiting a world from the past. As I found with my other books on Dwight Eisenhower and Ronald Reagan, nothing helps with the experience more than a trip to a presidential library—this time, a trip to the Franklin D. Roosevelt Presidential Library and Museum in Hyde Park, New York. It is located about forty miles north of West Point, above the Hudson River, and is a beautiful setting in all seasons. When I toured the grounds, I felt as if I was back in FDR's time. The stately family home, now showing the wear of age, is just a few yards from the museum, and walking the long driveway it's easy to picture Roosevelt, his legs shrunken by polio and encased in steel braces, struggling for hours at a time, trying to walk again. He never succeeded, but he also never stopped trying.

Driving the back roads of the property, one can imagine FDR doing the same in his 1936 Ford Phaeton convertible with special hand controls. He loved that car and often drove along the side roads and hills of Hyde Park, taking the curves at breakneck speed.

But the true work takes place in the reading room of the library, with its aged books lining the walls. There are over seventeen million documents in the FDR archives, and almost one million of them are available digitally. But there is something special about being there and holding the documents in your hands. Unlike at the Eisenhower Library, gloves are not required. The archivists thought gloves would make it hard to turn pages, which is true. In the library are the drafts of speeches, always of special interest to me, with edits scribbled in Roosevelt's hand; the urgent cables at critical moments of the war; and the correspondence between the president and Winston Churchill and Joseph Stalin, some of the letters in longhand. Collected in bound books are the records of the Tehran Conference with Churchill and Stalin, the centerpiece of this book. The firsthand accounts of observers and translators give readers a sense of being in the room as the three men fiercely debated the wisdom of a cross-Channel invasion on Western Europe. Trying to put the reader in the room is what the Three Days series is all about.

Much has been written about this period. A staff member at the FDR Library told me he thought Roosevelt was the most written-about person in American history, and I can understand why he'd think that. Many great historians have explored aspects of his life and contribution. I don't aspire to match the genius of historians, but intend to put my personal journalist's spin on the great events of Roosevelt's day. I am not a historian. I am a reporter of history. And this book, like the other two in the series, hopefully sheds light on a crucial moment in time and one of America's most important leaders.

As the third book in my presidential series, *Three Days at the Brink: FDR's Daring Gamble to Win World War II* rounds out the story of twentieth-century leadership and is a dramatic prelude to my other books—President Dwight D. Eisenhower at the early, most dangerous days of the Cold War, with Stalin breaking all the promises he'd made to Roosevelt; and President Ronald Reagan, bringing an end to the Cold War with dramatic diplomatic strategy alongside his Soviet counterpart, Mikhail Gorbachev. Like Eisenhower and Reagan, Roosevelt was a leader who rose above his political party to fulfill a higher purpose in the presidency. Looking at it today, with fresh problems around the world, it can feel as if in one way or another we're still having the same debates—still focused on a worldview from seventy-five years ago. In the living history of our times, we study the past to create a better future.

Bret Baier
October 2019

Prologue

THE "BIG THREE" DINNER PARTY
NOVEMBER 28, 1943

THE FUTURE WAS UNCERTAIN. After more than four years of fighting, it was not clear which side would win World War II. Hitler's armies had surged across Western Europe into Russia and the Mediterranean. The Allies had fought hard and scored some important victories, but they could not afford to miscalculate against an enemy so undaunted by defeat, so relentless in the face of overwhelming odds. They needed the kind of decisive win that would put the Nazis on their heels.

President Franklin D. Roosevelt, British prime

minister Winston Churchill, and Soviet marshal Joseph Stalin—the "Big Three" leaders of the Allied countries—met in Tehran, Iran, to try to figure out how to navigate this crisis point in World War II. Each of the three came with his own vision of the future. Stalin insisted that a second front be opened in Europe as soon as possible. Churchill didn't agree; he thought the Mediterranean would be a better place to fight. FDR was in the middle, leaning toward Stalin's view, but unsure on the question of timing. One thing was clear: the next great battle was on the horizon, and those three days in Tehran would determine its course. Hitler could still win the war. How would they stop him?

They knew they had to work together, but it was an uneasy alliance. Churchill felt he deserved accommodation since Britain had held off the Nazis virtually alone in the early years of the war. Stalin argued that Russia had suffered a true invasion of its land, costing millions of lives, and a second front would relieve the pressure on the war-weary Soviets.

FDR, who was meeting Stalin for the first time, was determined to show the Soviet leader a full measure of respect, even if his attentiveness hurt Churchill's feelings. Roosevelt had been trying to meet with Stalin for more than a year. He wanted Stalin's support in the war with Japan, which America was fighting mostly alone, with limited help from Britain.

The urgency of the meeting could not be overstated. If the Big Three did not reach an agreement, the Allied effort could falter. They needed a united policy at a time when the Soviets were fighting for their lives and Hitler's domination of Western Europe had remained largely unchallenged.

From the beginning, the three leaders did not see eye to eye. The conference was extremely difficult to set up, and it almost didn't happen. Stalin insisted that the meeting be held in Tehran. He argued that he needed to be close to home because of his duties there. Roosevelt countered that he could not be so far away and out of touch with Congress during this critical time, and the rough, mountainous terrain made it difficult for cables to be sent and received. Stalin held firm. Eventually, when it became clear he would not attend a conference if it were not in Tehran, Roosevelt folded.

The leaders also disagreed about where to meet in Tehran. Originally, Roosevelt had planned to meet at the American embassy, although it was not a large facility. Churchill offered the British embassy as an alternative. Stalin argued that the safest place to meet would be the fortresslike Soviet embassy, explaining that Soviet police had just arrested several of Hitler's agents, who were plotting an assassination attempt on the Big Three. They could not be sure that one or more of the assassins had not escaped into the hills, where they could move forward with the planned attack.

The risk of assassination was real. The meeting represented what Churchill called "the greatest concentration of power the world had ever seen." If any one of the three leaders were harmed, the result would be chaos. After twenty years in power, Stalin had no natural heir. The death of Churchill or Roosevelt would create a messy political aftermath, which would slow the momentum of the war.

Ultimately, the three agreed to meet at the Soviet embassy. It was lavish in appearance, but not very comfortable. The Americans knew that their rooms were bugged, and Roosevelt avoided saying anything he wouldn't mind having overheard. Stalin often popped into the president's office to see that all was well, like an overly attentive but not entirely trustworthy hotel manager. Members of Roosevelt's entourage also noticed that the maids, waiters, and bellmen all had bulges at their hips that appeared to be firearms, and suspected they were members of the NKVD, Stalin's secret police.

At the conference, Roosevelt, Churchill, and Stalin met together for the first time. FDR and Stalin had sized each other up in a private meeting earlier that afternoon. Their conversation, conducted through Stalin's translator, was cordial. Roosevelt thought the two of them would get along fine. Stalin was impressed by Roosevelt's powerful personality and intellect, and he felt humbled when he saw the extent of his infirmity. He realized how difficult it must have been for the wheelchair-bound president to make the journey of thousands of miles by sea and air. He graciously promised Roosevelt that their next meeting would be in a more convenient setting for the president—a promise he broke when he demanded Yalta, on the Black Sea, even farther from America, for their second summit.

For his part, Roosevelt was surprised to see that Stalin was short—only five feet six—and stocky, with broad shoulders and an expansive waist. He was pleasant, even witty, but his eyes were impossible to read and his mouth was masked behind his thick mustache. Roosevelt set out to court the Soviet leader, knowing that he needed his support for the fight in Japan.

At the dinner hour, Roosevelt arrived in the dining room before the others, to avoid being wheeled in as they watched. There was tension during their dinner. Churchill seemed irked as Roosevelt charmed Stalin, even calling him "Uncle Joe." He understood that the president was trying to win Stalin over, but he bristled that the jokes were often at his expense.

In the coming days, the greatest questions of the war would be debated: Where was the next front going to be? Would they cross the English Channel and land in France—and would they do it soon, as Stalin was urging? Did they have the troops and the air and sea power to make the push? The English Channel had blocked German advances in World War I, and even Hitler, at his boldest in 1940, had not crossed the Channel to invade Britain. If they went ahead, which American general had the skill to serve as supreme commander of that mission? Could they summon the nerve and the resources for an operation whose success could win the war, but whose failure could mean defeat?

Beneath the strategizing, there was the underlying question: Could they trust one another? Could they afford *not* to? Each of the Big Three had based their actions on national priorities, but now they needed to act as one.

The story of this vital conference provides an inside view of the intimate interactions of great powers at a perilous time in history. Their debates would range from the profound to the petty, from the emotional to the calculated. Each of the leaders felt the weight of history, but only time would tell how deeply their decisions affected the shape of the world, for both good and ill.

Through it all, Roosevelt was the lead strategist for the

future, the man who could shape their place in history. Alone in his private quarters, Roosevelt worried about his master strategy and the practical issues of working with a man like Stalin. The president felt uneasy about Stalin's ruthless grip on power, his bloody regime that exiled or murdered his personal and political enemies, and his dictatorial control over his people. Clearly Stalin was a transactional leader; he sought relations with the Western powers because he needed them to defeat Hitler. But could he be a reliable partner? Roosevelt wanted to give Stalin the benefit of the doubt, to see him as a collaborator in building a free and equal world. The president trusted his adviser Harry Hopkins, who assured him Stalin only wanted safety and prosperity for his people, as any leader might.

In the stifling quarters of the Soviet embassy, Roosevelt considered the future. He wanted to build a partnership with Stalin without giving him room to grow stronger. He knew he could not leave Tehran without a plan. In this watershed moment of the war, it was time to make a daring gamble.

It was a challenge he had been preparing for all his life.

PART ONE

THE MAKING OF FDR

1

TO WHOM MUCH IS GIVEN

FRANKLIN DELANO ROOSEVELT WAS groomed by his mother to be far more than a country gentleman at his Hyde Park, New York, estate. Indeed, Sara Roosevelt would live to see her son elected president of the United States not once but three times before her death. (He was elected to a fourth term after she died.)

Roosevelt was a complex person. One of the central questions about his life was how he came to be the champion of the common folk. Americans often see themselves reflected in their popular leaders, particularly those with humble roots, yet FDR grew up in a wealthy family. But he was crippled by polio just as his political life was taking off, and this crisis did a lot to form his style and philosophy. Instead of being devastated, Roosevelt's illness and subsequent paralysis of his legs gave him a depth and purpose that he did not have before. As political commentator George Will put it, "Just as the irons were clamped on his legs, the steel entered his soul."

FDR was a natural leader. He was optimistic, charming, confident, strong-willed, and he had the ability to communicate clearly and passionately. He was also flawed. He could be remote, self-indulgent, and careless with those who loved him most. But at the time he became president, his strengths inspired the nation. Stunned by the Great Depression, weighed down with debt and despair, Americans found in Roosevelt a man who gave them a reason to hope.

Franklin Delano Roosevelt was born on January 30, 1882, at the family estate in Hyde Park, to James and Sara Delano Roosevelt. The couple had married two years earlier. At age twenty-six, Sara never expected to marry; her family money allowed her the freedom to travel the world and do as she pleased. James, a fifty-two-year-old widower, had graduated from Harvard Law School, but hated being a lawyer. Instead, he focused on business and investments and lived as a country gentleman, dabbling in local affairs while enjoying his boating and horse stables. He lived happily with his first wife and their son, James Roosevelt Roosevelt (the double last name used instead of Jr.), who was known as Rosy. His first wife died at age forty-five from a heart attack.

James had no plans to remarry, but four years after his wife's death he met the beautiful daughter of his friend Warren Delano. The couple fell in love, and despite the twenty-six-year age difference, they married. After Franklin was born, the family settled into the estate at Hyde Park. It was a beautiful setting, high above the Hudson River, a retreat from the world where Sara could nurture her son, who became the great love and chief occupation of her life.

Sara was committed to her son's intellectual, emotional, and character development. She believed children were essentially small adults who lacked the vocabulary to express their thoughts. She thought that he could expand his vocabulary by reading, so Sara encouraged Franklin's interest in books. He became obsessed with history, especially naval history, a passion that would last his lifetime.

Franklin spent a lot of time with adults. His only sibling was his adult half brother, Rosy, so he was basically raised as an only child. Franklin was homeschooled by governesses and tutors until age fourteen. Sara realized Franklin was sheltered, but she never thought he was lonely. Endlessly curious, he had a gift for making an adventure out of any situation. "I do not believe I have ever seen a little boy who seemed always to be so consistently enjoying himself," she wrote.

Even though he spent a lot of time alone, Franklin liked being with other children, and he naturally took on the role of leader when they played games. When Sara saw Franklin ordering his playmates around, she suggested he give others a turn at command. "Mummie," he replied, "if I didn't give the orders, nothing would happen."

His father took him on adventures—sailing the Hudson River, horseback riding, and shooting. The family also traveled extensively. In his first fourteen years, Franklin visited Europe eight times.

When Franklin was fourteen, his parents decided he needed more formal schooling, so they enrolled him at Groton School, an elite Massachusetts boarding academy. The school focused on simple living, religious observance, physical exercise, and devotion to the public good. As a new student, he had to establish himself with other boys who had been together since they were twelve. He never complained in his letters home, easing his mother's fears.

Franklin loved sports but failed to make the football or baseball teams. Instead, he was the manager of the baseball team, organizing equipment and being at the beck and call of the players. He didn't whine about it, and his lack of self-pity earned the respect of his classmates.

He didn't particularly distinguish himself with his teachers. Decades later, when Franklin was president, one of his instructors wrote a positive but less than glowing evaluation of the boy he knew at Groton: "The fact is—from my remembrance—Franklin was colorless; a nice, pleasant boy who did not get into trouble and did do as he should. But remained submerged."

Franklin had always been taught to help those who were less fortunate. He joined the Groton Missionary Society to do charitable works. He helped an eighty-four-year-old black woman—the widow of a Civil War drummer—by plowing her driveway when it snowed, feeding her chickens, and stocking her coal bin. On a couple of occasions, he also worked two-week sessions at the Missionary Society's New Hampshire summer camp for poor children.

He spent most of his summers at Campobello, a small island off the coast of Maine, where the family had a house. There he developed a passion for golf. He built a golf course on the island and started an annual tournament. The island's other residents didn't entirely see the point of sectioning off such pristine grassland, so often the golfers had to dodge grazing sheep. He remained an avid golfer well into adulthood, and those who played with him said he had a powerful swing and an ability to hit long drives.

After graduating from Groton, Franklin went to Harvard College in 1900. He sang with the glee club and became active in politics. Although his side of the Roosevelt family were Democrats, Franklin supported his Republican cousin Theodore, who had been nominated for vice president on William McKinley's ticket. Franklin joined the Republican Club, and when the McKinley-Roosevelt ticket won, he joined his classmates at a victory parade in Boston.

Not long after, Franklin learned that his seventy-two-year-old father had suffered a heart attack. His mother assured Franklin that he was recuperating in New York City. But as the weeks went on, Franklin grew frustrated by the slow course of his father's recovery. Agonizing, he wrote to his parents, "I am too distressed about Papa and cannot understand why he does not improve more quickly." James did not improve. Finally, in early December, a telegram arrived from Sara: the situation was dire; Franklin must come to New York. He was by his father's side when he died on December 8, 1900. Grief stricken, Sara clung to her son. In 1902 and 1903, she rented a house in Boston so that she could be close to him during the school year.

Throughout his time at Harvard, Franklin worked at the school newspaper, the *Crimson*. He wasn't chosen at first, but a bit of daring and family connection earned him a major scoop and a position on the staff. In April 1901, Franklin learned from a family member about a secret visit to Harvard being planned by his cousin Theodore, now vice president. He was to speak to the constitutional government class of his friend Professor Abbott Lawrence Lowell. Franklin wrote about a surprise appearance planned for the following day, and two thousand students showed up outside Lowell's classroom to meet the vice president.

The summer after her husband died, Sara said she could not bear to go to Campobello, so she took Franklin to Europe. On the trip home, they learned that President McKinley had been assassinated, and Cousin Teddy was now the twenty-sixth president of the United States.

Franklin admired his cousin. He seemed larger than life, although he stood only five feet ten inches tall. He had tremendous energy and was physically fearless in a manner that could take a young boy's breath away. He was a loving, engaged father to his six children—one by his first wife, Alice, and five more by his second wife, Edith. People were captivated by his sincerity and by the joy he took in everything he did. Even though he and Franklin were of different political parties, they shared so many of the same beliefs that the term "Roosevelt Republican" was later coined to describe progressives. To Franklin, Cousin Teddy represented the new century, with goals of economic equity, conservation, military strength, and globalization.

Franklin dated a number of women in college, but he kept this part of his life secret from his mother. Then he became interested in his fifth cousin once removed, Anna Eleanor Roosevelt (called Eleanor), who was the niece of President Roosevelt. They had seen each other at family functions since they were small children but didn't know each other well. In the summer of 1902, as Franklin rode the train from New York City to Hyde Park, he happened to see Eleanor on the train and stopped to talk. He was so interested in their conversation that he stayed for an hour, and then he invited Eleanor to come and say hello to his mother.

Months later, Franklin saw Eleanor again at a family event, and he began to ask her out for tea and coffee. Franklin was dazzled by Eleanor's proximity to the president he admired so deeply, but he was also drawn to her personality. He saw beneath her shy manner a warmth that touched him, and also an open-minded interest in the world.

Eleanor had had a difficult childhood. She was the daughter of Theodore Roosevelt's younger brother, Elliott, and Anna Rebecca Hall, a leading socialite of the era. Eleanor had a strained relationship with her mother, who was often critical of Eleanor's shyness and plain appearance. Her mother died of diphtheria—a bacterial infection—when Eleanor was eight. Her father was an alcoholic who committed suicide when Eleanor was ten. Eleanor and her younger brother lived with their maternal grandmother, who was strict and unaffectionate.

At fifteen, Eleanor escaped her grandmother's rigid household when she was sent to a finishing school in London. For the first time she had friends and people who appreciated her. Eleanor was encouraged to speak up for herself; she blossomed and became more self-assured. She stood five feet eleven inches tall and had a slender build, with waist-length hair and clear blue eyes, but she was not conventionally beautiful.

Franklin and Eleanor kept their relationship secret from his mother throughout 1903. Franklin proposed to Eleanor on November 21, 1903; Eleanor accepted. FDR dreaded telling his mother about the engagement. He initially suggested that they keep their plans to themselves, but Eleanor saw no point to that. He would have to tell his mother eventually.

It would be a difficult conversation. Franklin knew his mother would be angry that he had not shared news of his relationship. Following the family Thanksgiving in 1903, Franklin took his mother aside and told her that he was in love with Cousin Eleanor and wanted to marry her. As feared, his mother was stunned and disapproved of the union. She considered the shy Eleanor a poor match for her charismatic son.

Sara also argued that at twenty-one and still in school, Franklin was not ready to marry. She urged him to take more time to consider. She assumed her son was inexperienced with women. "It probably surprised me only because he had never been in any sense a ladies' man," she wrote of Franklin's announcement. "I don't believe I remember ever hearing him talk about girls or even a girl . . ." It didn't occur to her that Franklin might have a side to his life of which she knew nothing.

Franklin's mother urged him to wait a year to make an announcement. She said that if at that time he still wanted to marry Eleanor, she would give the marriage her blessing. He agreed.

It was a difficult year. Eleanor distracted herself by working at the University Settlement House in New York, helping young immigrant women. Franklin attended school, and reluctantly agreed to take a world trip with his mother near the end of the year of waiting. To Sara's disappointment, the distance from Eleanor did not change his mind.

On October 11, 1904, Franklin gave Eleanor a diamond ring from Tiffany for her birthday. The engagement was officially announced on December 1.

Eleanor's uncle President Roosevelt wrote to Franklin, giving his blessing. "We are greatly rejoiced over the good news. I am as fond of Eleanor as if she were my daughter," he wrote, "and I like you, and trust you, and believe in you. No other success in life—not the Presidency, or anything else—begins to compare with the joy and happiness that come in and from the love of the true man and the true woman."

The wedding was scheduled for March 17, 1905, in New York City. The couple was delighted when the president, who planned to be in town for the Saint Patrick's Day parade, agreed to attend and give Eleanor away. Family and friends gathered in the spacious parlor of cousin Susie Parish's house on East Seventy-Sixth Street in New York City for the wedding. Eleanor looked lovely in her white satin gown, and she wore a pearl necklace, a gift from her mother-in-law.

President Roosevelt's presence overwhelmed the event, as crowds gathered on the street outside, hoping to catch a glimpse of the president. As his daughter Alice once said, "My father always has to be the bride at every wedding, the corpse at every funeral, and the baby at every christening." At the reception, Franklin and Eleanor stood alone in the receiving line; their guests were in the next room, crowding around the president and hanging on his every word.

After the reception was over, the newlyweds took the train to Hyde Park. Sara had given them free use of the house for the first week of their honeymoon. Their marriage was truly a meeting of the minds, but it never achieved the intimacy that Eleanor longed for. Franklin rarely shared his true thoughts and feelings with his wife.

In the early years of their marriage, Eleanor suffered from her husband's lack of attention. She entered a decade of almost constant pregnancy, giving birth to six children, under the controlling direction of her mother-in-law. Eleanor worried that she was an inadequate wife and mother, while Franklin launched the political career that would be his true passion.

2

INTO THE ARENA

EVEN THOUGH FRANKLIN ROOSEVELT wasn't very good at stump speeches at the beginning of his political career, the voters in upstate New York gave him a chance. He was, after all, a *Roosevelt*.

Roosevelt decided to run for the state senate in 1910 after three years practicing law in New York City. Franklin hated the legal grind. He felt called to public service, inspired by the forceful presidency of his cousin, whose second term had ended the year before. President Theodore Roosevelt had recently challenged people to take on the demands of citizenship, saying: "The credit belongs to the man who is actually in the arena . . . who spends himself in a worthy cause; who at the best knows in the end the triumph of high achievement, and who at the worst, if he fails, at least fails while daring greatly, so that his place shall never be with those cold and timid souls who neither know victory nor defeat."

FDR took his cousin's words to heart, accepting the challenge by running for political office. When the Dutchess County district attorney asked him to run for the Poughkeepsie state assembly seat being vacated by a sitting Democrat, Franklin decided it was the perfect place to start a political career. When the assemblyman changed his mind, Roosevelt chose to try for a state senate seat, even though Dutchess County had always been a Republican stronghold. The Democrats thought Roosevelt would be a party loyalist, but he wasn't. At the nominating convention, he made his stance clear: "I accept this nomination with absolute independence," he said. "I am pledged to no man; I am influenced by no special interests."

At twenty-eight, FDR wasn't a polished candidate, but he had a charm of his own. Teddy Roosevelt was delighted that his cousin was entering politics and never spoke a word against him. FDR campaigned against special interests and Tammany Hall, the Democratic political machine in New York City, which was known for corruption.

FDR campaigned tirelessly. Touring across the farmlands of upstate New York, he stopped to speak whenever he spotted a gathering of a few people. Once, he accidentally spent a few hours campaigning across the state line in Connecticut, only later realizing he'd been speaking to people who couldn't vote for him.

"What the voters have got to do is to clean their house this year," he said in an October speech. "They are going to discharge the unfaithful servant, and they are going to put in a new servant who stands for cleanliness, honesty and economy." To the shock of the establishment, FDR won. He might not have shaken *every* constituent's hand, but he certainly tried.

Once elected, Roosevelt moved his family to Albany, the state capital, an unusual thing to do because the legislature met for less than three months a year. FDR wanted his constituents to see him hard at work for them every day of the year.

For Eleanor, the move freed her from the watchful eye of her mother-in-law. The early years of her marriage had been consumed by childbirth—Anna in 1906, James in 1907, Franklin Jr. (who died in infancy) in 1909, and Elliott, born weeks before the election in 1910. She had a home of her own for the first time. "I wanted to be independent," Eleanor wrote in her memoir about that period. "I was beginning to realize that something within me craved to be an individual."

In the senate, FDR didn't waste any time making his mark. The first controversy involved the appointment of a United States senator. In those days, senators were elected by state legislatures. (This system would change in 1913 with the passage of the Seventeenth Amendment, calling for the popular election of US senators.) The party chose a well-connected Democrat, rather than the best person for the job. Roosevelt considered it his duty as a representative of upstate New York to reject the influence of New York City and the political establishment. He and his supporters won the fight, and FDR claimed a moral victory, even though the replacement was equally tied to special interests.

His own party complained that FDR was an elitist snob. Some wondered if the Democratic Party would turn against him. Others recognized potential greatness in the young politician. One man who supported FDR from the start was newspaperman Louis McHenry Howe, a freelance political reporter for the *New York Herald*. Howe was an odd character; he was a petite chain smoker with a high forehead and prominent buck teeth. Howe immediately fell for FDR. "I was so impressed by Franklin Roosevelt . . . almost at that very first meeting," Howe said. "I made up my mind that he was Presidential timber and that nothing but an accident could keep him from becoming President of the United States."

Howe saw FDR's potential. He worked his way into FDR's circle, teaching him the ropes and showing him how to stand his ground. Howe became one of FDR's most important strategists. At that early point, FDR's key ideas were borrowed from his cousin. He didn't yet know what he stood for, except the general sense that he wanted to be a fair representative to his constituents. He was a good listener and the people he represented sensed his sincerity.

FDR loved the political whirlwind, the heated debates, and the exchange of ideas. He was thinking about issues in a new way and becoming progressive, even as Eleanor held back. She was slow to embrace pro-women issues of the day. Neither she nor her mother-in-law believed that women should vote, but when FDR announced his support for the suffrage movement, Eleanor went along. "I realized that if my husband were a suffragist, I must be, too," she wrote.

FDR ran for reelection in 1912 and won. Cousin Teddy decided to run for the Republican nomination against the sitting president, William Howard Taft. He had helped Taft win, but he had grown disillusioned by Taft's failure to advance a reform agenda. He lost the nomination but launched an independent candidacy. "I'm as strong as a bull moose," he told an audience, and his progressive party became known as the Bull Moose Party.

As a Democratic state senator, Franklin supported the Democratic candidate, Woodrow Wilson. It was the first time two Roosevelts were positioned against each other in an important election, but both men knew it was a political necessity.

While making a campaign speech in Milwaukee, Teddy was shot in the chest in an assassination attempt. The bullet hit the former president's glasses case and a wad of speech papers in his vest before entering his body. Teddy paused, then continued his speech: "Friends, I shall ask you to be as quiet as possible. I don't know whether you fully understand that I have just been shot; but it takes more than that to kill a Bull Moose . . . The bullet is in me now, so that I cannot make a very long speech, but I will try my best." He then spoke for ninety minutes! The bullet remained in his chest for the rest of his life. Despite Teddy's heroic efforts on the campaign trail, Wilson won the election.

Wilson chose Josephus Daniels, a newspaper editor and campaign supporter, who had little knowledge of the navy or the sea, to serve as secretary of the navy.

When FDR and Eleanor attended Wilson's inauguration, Daniels pulled FDR aside. "Would you like to come to Washington as assistant secretary?" Daniels asked him. "I'd like it bully well," FDR replied with a grin.

FDR loved his new position. With 65,000 men and a budget of $150 million under his direction, he thought he could make a difference in assuring America's military strength. "I was very pleased to hear you were appointed assistant secretary of the navy," Teddy Roosevelt wrote to his cousin. "It is interesting to see that you are at another place which I myself once held." FDR had a lot to learn because he had never been in the military.

In Washington, Eleanor found herself swept into social obligations, visiting the wives of important people in government. It didn't come naturally to her, but Eleanor grew into the role. When she became pregnant for the fifth time, she hired a secretary, a lovely, soft-spoken, and well-educated young woman named Lucy Mercer.

With his job, FDR was able to spend time at home with his family; his children adored him. He was gentle with his "chicks" and a lousy disciplinarian. The task of discipline was left to Eleanor, who didn't like being a disciplinarian, either, but was forced into the role. Their son James recounted one occasion when the rebellious little Elliott did something so egregious that it warranted his father's attention. Elliott, full of fear, was taken by his mother to FDR's study. FDR sat him on his knee, put his arm around him, and proceeded to chat gently with him about a variety of things, never mentioning his transgression.

"In half an hour Mother came back and said, 'Is everything settled?'

"Father replied, 'Everything is settled.'"

In his position with the navy, FDR was not yet burdened with the conflicts afflicting Europe and East Asia. The situation overseas was tense. There was unrest in a number of colonies, and many empires had pledged to support each other in the event of war. The United States was not involved in these imperial power structures, and most people dismissed them as Old World disputes that had little to do with America.

War seemed inevitable. The fighting broke out in 1914 when Archduke Franz Ferdinand of Austria was assassinated in Sarajevo. Austria declared war on Serbia, with the support of Germany. Russia countered in defense of Serbia, and the war was on. Within a month, the alliances were in force, with Germany declaring war on France and Belgium; Austria on Russia and Belgium; France and Britain on Austria; and Japan on Germany. Ultimately, the war was configured into two forces: the Central Powers—Germany, Austria-Hungary, the

Ottoman Empire, and Bulgaria—and the Allied Powers—France, the British Empire, Italy, Russia, and Japan.

FDR thought the United States should add its might to the fight against Germany and the Central Powers, but Wilson didn't want to get involved. "The United States must be neutral in fact as well as in name during these days that are to try men's souls," he declared.

Unconvinced, FDR wondered if he could make a difference as an elected official. There was an open seat for the US Senate in New York, and he decided to run, although he did not resign from his position as assistant secretary of the navy. He was wise to have kept his day job, because he was defeated in the primary.

FDR was distraught to see America sitting on the sidelines during the Great War. He pushed to improve America's naval readiness, but his efforts were dismissed by Wilson. The folly of this position became clear in 1915 when the Germans announced that any ship caught in the waters around Britain would be torpedoed, even if it was a passenger or commercial ship from the neutral United States. When several small commercial ships were attacked, the Wilson administration did nothing. Then the Germans attacked a British ocean liner, the RMS *Lusitania*, which was traveling from New York to Liverpool with 1,959 people on board; 128 Americans died.

The calls for the United States to enter the war grew

louder. FDR hoped that Wilson noticed. He felt discouraged when Wilson campaigned for reelection with the slogan, "He kept us out of war."

Wilson narrowly won reelection. Two weeks after his inauguration, the Germans torpedoed three American merchant ships. On April 2, Wilson called together a joint session of Congress to declare war.

FDR wanted to enlist in the service and go to the front, but was told his service with the navy was too important to the war effort. His primary job was to oversee tens of thousands of civilian employees, including the difficult job of dealing with the labor unions.

Eleanor also felt called to serve. Her fifth child, also named Franklin Jr. after her second son, who died in infancy, had been born in 1914, and her sixth and final child, John, in 1916. "For ten years I was always just getting over having a baby or about to have one," she said, "and so my occupations were considerably restricted." She became a volunteer for the Red Cross with her assistant Lucy Mercer by her side, organizing canteens that would serve free hot meals to soldiers on their way to the front, and visiting the war wounded, whose terrible injuries and haunted eyes had a profound effect on her.

Eager to experience war firsthand, FDR visited the front lines in France during the summer of 1918. While FDR was traveling aboard the destroyer USS *Dyer*,

Teddy Roosevelt's son Quentin, serving with the Army Air Service's Ninety-Fifth Aero Squadron, was shot down over France. The Germans were shocked to learn they'd killed President Theodore Roosevelt's son. In a rare moment of respect on the battlefield, they buried him with military honors and erected a cross inscribed, "Lieutenant Roosevelt, Buried by the Germans." Teddy's other sons, Archie and Theodore Jr., were in France recovering from war wounds. FDR was frustrated that he was not in uniform while these brave Roosevelts were so courageously going into battle.

In France, FDR toured several battlefields. The devastation made a deep impression on him. Decades later, in 1936, while campaigning for his second term as president, FDR recalled his time in France while vowing to keep America out of another European war. He had not *seen* war, but he had seen its aftermath: "I have seen war . . . I have seen blood running from the wounded. I have seen men coughing out their gassed lungs. I have seen the dead in the mud. I have seen cities destroyed . . . I have seen children starving. I have seen the agony of mothers and wives. I hate war."

When he returned home, FDR fell ill with double pneumonia. He had to be carried off the ship on a stretcher. Eleanor brought him home and tucked him into bed while she began unpacking his luggage. There she found a bundle of love letters from Lucy Mercer, her assistant. Eleanor was crushed. She had never suspected the affair, although it wasn't a surprise to others.

Eleanor knew her handsome husband was flirtatious, and she had always been afraid she was no match for him. But she had assumed he would not break his wedding vows. Now that he had, how could their marriage continue? She offered to divorce him. She also told his mother, who was outraged on Eleanor's behalf.

Divorce was not an option for Franklin. His mother would cut off his funds, and divorce would end his political career. In addition, FDR loved his family and did not want to leave them. His relationship with Eleanor was not very romantic, despite the fact that Eleanor addressed her letters to him "Dearest Honey," and he affectionately called her "Babs," and while away would write, "I long so to be with you." He may have fallen in love with Lucy Mercer, but his love for his wife existed on a different plane. He could not see himself living without her. So, he made amends as best he could and vowed to never see Lucy again—a promise he did not keep. Eleanor would never get over it. There was no mention of the affair in her memoirs, but she confided her deep misery to those closest to her.

As FDR and Eleanor struggled to repair their marriage, they were relieved by the declaration of peace on November 11. In the end, Germany was forced to give up its arsenal and some territories and pay $37 billion in reparations. These humiliating conditions fueled a rage among the German population that would grow into a movement to restore German greatness, the origins of Nazism.

In June 1920, Eleanor vacationed with the children while FDR attended the Democratic National Convention in San Francisco. She didn't know that FDR's name had been placed in nomination for vice president of the United States on the ticket of James M. Cox, the governor of Ohio.

The Democratic platform was one FDR could get behind: it supported Wilson's League of Nations, as well as women's suffrage. Earlier that month, the Nineteenth Amendment, giving women the right to vote, had been passed by Congress, and it would go on to be ratified on August 18. In the November election, eight million women would cast votes.

FDR's nomination wasn't a surprise. He had been quietly campaigning for months, and Cox respected him. FDR was delighted to be on the ticket, and he resigned his job with the navy to campaign.

The Republicans nominated Ohio senator Warren Harding, who vowed to campaign against Wilson's League of Nations and for a return to normalcy. He argued that the nation was tired of progressives like

Teddy Roosevelt and Wilson. He promised to put "America first," arguing that "Independence means independence, now as in 1776." The approach appealed to war-weary Americans.

On Election Day, Harding won the White House with the largest popular vote margin ever recorded. FDR reconsidered his political future. He was as committed as ever to building a new and stronger Democratic Party—but how?

Up to this point, FDR's political climb had been steady: election to state government, service in a presidential administration, a place on a national ticket. Everyone talked about his family connections, his attractive qualities, his hard work, but few could identify his compelling reason for being in the arena. He was thoughtful but not driven, political but not particularly idealistic. He had never faced a serious personal crisis.

That changed almost overnight in the summer of 1921. FDR was used to asserting a cool control over his life and ambitions, but he was powerless when it came to one obstacle: a crippling disease known as polio.

3

POLIO

IN THE MONTHS AFTER the election, Franklin Roosevelt took a break from politics. In August 1921, he joined his family at their summer house on Campobello Island in Maine. One afternoon, he swam with the children at a swimming pond, then jogged two miles back to the house. He didn't feel right.

Normally, he loved those jogs from the swimming pond, but that day, something was off. He didn't feel "the glow I'd expected." When he reached the house, the mail was in with several newspapers and he sat reading for a while, "too tired even to dress. I'd never felt quite that way before." Soon he announced that he was too tired to eat dinner and went straight to bed. He thought he might be coming down with a cold.

The next morning, he woke with a 102-degree fever and excruciating pain in the backs of his legs. Eleanor called for the local doctor, who examined him and said he had a bad summer cold. The pain kept getting worse, and by the next day FDR was paralyzed from the waist down.

After consulting several doctors, FDR was diagnosed with poliomyelitis—polio—an infectious disease that attacks the central nervous system. While the disease usually afflicts children, it can sometimes attack adults. At first, FDR was optimistic, expecting the paralysis to be temporary. Although he regained the full use of his upper body, FDR's legs remained paralyzed for the rest of his life.

He refused to give up his belief that he would recover. The family returned to New York City so FDR could be close to his doctors. Newspaper headlines described his condition, and many reporters assumed his political career was over.

Early in his recovery, the children were kept away from their father, due to concerns that they might contract polio from him. They were told very little. When the danger of infection had passed, FDR was determined to ease his children's fears, to show them they had not lost their father. Whenever they entered his room, he made an effort to laugh and joke with them, and demanded that they tell him every detail of their lives. FDR eased their worries by talking matter-of-factly about his condition, and he let them see his legs.

James, who was attending school at Groton, remembered coming home for Christmas full of dread about seeing his crippled father. But when he entered the room, "Pa read me like a book, and he worked a small miracle for me. He was propped up on pillows, and those trapezes and rings over his bed on which he already was exercising his upper body upset me a bit. Pa instantly made me forget it. His chin still stuck out and he was grinning and he stretched out his arms to me. 'Come here, old man!' he said." James rushed into his father's arms and discovered that the familiar powerful arms had not been wasted by the disease. He cried a little, but then within moments they were chatting merrily about Groton.

Roosevelt's loyal aide, Louis Howe, had planned to retire from politics, but now he felt called to a higher mission. "This is my job," he told Eleanor. "Helping Franklin." He moved into the family home in New York City. Howe and Eleanor both realized that for FDR to heal, he would need to follow his ambitions and live a vital life.

His mother wanted her son to retire at Hyde Park. She considered Howe the enemy because he wanted to drag her fragile son back into public life. Eleanor stood with Howe. She knew that sentencing her husband to a useless life would be like pounding a nail into his coffin. She fought for him. "The day of the timid, fluttering, inept housewife, subservient to the whims of her husband and her mother-in-law, was over," James later remembered.

"I hoped he would devote himself to his restoration of health and to the writing perhaps of the books he had always longed to get on paper," Sara Roosevelt wrote in her memoir about FDR. "But Franklin had no intention of conforming to my quiet ideas for his future existence. He was determined to ignore his disability and carry on from where he had left off."

FDR worked ceaselessly on his recovery. He received advice from other polio sufferers, including recommendations to use swimming in warm water as therapy. He tried it and found that being in a pool restored him to his upright self. He spent six weeks at a spa in Warm Springs, Georgia, where the mineral waters were thought to be healing, swimming for hours at a time without tiring.

From then on, the spa became like a second home to FDR. He felt at ease with his fellow "polios." In that setting, he didn't have to be ashamed of his shriveled legs or apologize for what he could no longer do. He thrived in his role as teacher and leader. He enjoyed inspiring and teaching young children and adults, and they gave him the nickname Dr. Roosevelt, which delighted him.

Back at Hyde Park, FDR continued his rehabilitation, determined to walk again. With his legs in heavy steel braces and leaning on crutches, he made his way down the long driveway, never actually standing on his feet, but swiveling one leg to the next and propelling himself forward by force of his upper-body strength. It was exhausting, leaving him drenched in sweat. After two years of work, doctors thoroughly examined his muscles and found that he had made no real progress.

FDR's body never recovered, but mentally, he rose above his limitations. In many ways, the setback strengthened him, giving him a challenge big enough to match his ambitions. His paralysis was a tragedy, but it also made him a better man. He developed qualities he'd never had before—patience, determination, reliance on others, and empathy.

He developed the upper-body strength of a bodybuilder; his arms could lift his entire weight when necessary. His face filled out, becoming heavier and livelier. His lower body withered; his legs were sometimes supported by steel braces that would allow him to inch along if he could hold on to something or someone for support. He could even give the appearance of walking, but he never actually walked again.

FDR had to reshape his view of the world and of his ability, but for the most part he refused to see his limitations. "He steadfastly refused to concede even to himself that he was functioning under a handicap and to this day I don't believe any one has ever heard him make any reference to his illness," his mother wrote. "I know I never have."

FDR had stayed close to Al Smith, who was reelected governor of New York in 1922. Smith was running for president, and he asked FDR to give his nominating speech at the Democratic National Convention, which was being held at Madison Square Garden in New York City on June 24, 1924.

Roosevelt refused to be pushed onstage in a wheelchair. He asked his son to escort him and lend an arm. FDR had developed a system for moving in an upright position relying on a strong crutch under one arm and an even stronger human prop on the other side holding him up. His legs were locked into braces to hold them steady and he used his powerful arms to support himself.

FDR and his son James practiced the fifteen-foot walk to the podium many times. On the day of the speech, they made their way slowly across the stage, FDR beaming as if he didn't have a care in the world. When they reached the podium, the audience erupted in applause. Here was the man they had always known, standing tall. When he began to speak, his powerful voice rumbled across the hall, as commanding as ever. Smith lost the nomination—and ultimately the Democrats lost the election—but FDR emerged as the hero of the convention.

He didn't mind giving the audience the false impression that he could stand and walk. FDR hated the pity he received, and he resented being dismissed as if he no longer had anything of value to offer. If he could find a way to help people see him for who he really was on the inside by manipulating their view of the outside, so be it. The convention appearance marked the beginning of FDR's comeback to the public stage.

Eleanor wasn't sure about her husband's chances. "Do you really believe that Franklin has a political future?" Eleanor asked Howe.

"I believe someday Franklin will be president," he said.

Howe thought the best thing for FDR was to keep his name and ideas in the forefront. He encouraged

Eleanor to get out in public and make political contacts of her own. She became close friends with Nancy Cook and Marion Dickerman, and the three women spent time together at Hyde Park. FDR built a cottage for the women on the Val-Kill stream; for the first time, Eleanor had a place of her own. Eleanor began earning her own income, by giving lectures, writing magazine articles, and appearing on radio broadcasts.

In 1927, FDR decided to buy the spa in Georgia and turn it into a rehabilitation facility. Almost nobody in his inner circle thought it was a good idea, including Eleanor, who was concerned about the high cost of putting their children through school. But he was determined, and the Georgia Warm Springs Foundation for Infantile Paralysis was created. FDR called it his greatest legacy.

In 1928, Al Smith planned to run for president again. He wanted FDR to succeed him as governor of New York. FDR wasn't sure he wanted the job. He felt he needed more time for rehabilitation before he ran for office. He was at the spa in Georgia when he was nominated by unanimous agreement. FDR accepted.

Howe wasn't pleased. He thought FDR should wait until 1932 for his comeback, first as governor of New York and then as a candidate for president in 1936.

Smith dismissed worries about Roosevelt's physical abilities. "The governor does not have to be an acrobat," he said. "We do not elect him for his ability to do a double back flip or a handspring."

FDR wanted to project the right image of authority. He asked photographers not to take pictures of him being carried from his car, and the press complied.

It turned out FDR was fit to run. He campaigned with the same fierce energy shown in the campaigns of his youth, visiting every one of New York's sixty-two counties. He learned all he could about New York politics.

FDR doubted that the Democrats could win the White House in 1928, given the nation's state of prosperity. He was right: Republican Herbert Hoover defeated Smith. When FDR went to bed on election night, he thought that he had lost his race for governor, too. In the morning he found that he had narrowly won. He was back in the arena.

Smith expected to return to New York and work behind the scenes, almost as a shadow governor. He planned for his own people to be put in place, and he didn't expect FDR to be an active governor. But Roosevelt was determined to be his own man. He hired Samuel Rosenman as an adviser and speechwriter. Rosenman admired the way his boss checked in with both advisers and ordinary constituents, noting that FDR had a talent for making each visitor feel as though the governor's legislative success depended on input from that person. "Tell me," he'd say, "what would you recommend if you were governor?"

As governor, faced with a Republican legislature and critical newspaper coverage, FDR decided to take his case directly to the people. In 1929, he began addressing his constituents in "fireside chats" over the radio, an outreach he would continue throughout his presidency.

"I am very mindful of the fact that I am the governor, not just of the Democrats, but of Republicans and all other citizens of the state," FDR said in a fireside chat in 1929. "That is why this talk . . . will be just as much as I can make [it] nonpartisan in character. I want merely to state facts and leave the people of the state to draw their own conclusions."

The politics of the nation changed overnight when the stock market crashed on October 24, 1929. The economic collapse wiped out the prosperity of the 1920s and sent the nation reeling. It triggered a worldwide economic depression that would continue for a decade.

In the early days after the crash, President Hoover tried to paint a hopeful picture, promising that the strong economy could shoulder the blow. In his first public address on the crisis a month later, President Hoover urged the country to rise above despair. Within the year, the full impact of the Depression had spread to nearly every household. Unemployment had risen from 3.14 percent to 8.67 percent; it would reach nearly 25 percent by 1932.

First, the crisis hit the farm communities and the working poor, then it spread to the middle class. Even those who had jobs found their paychecks cut to poverty wages. People did anything to raise cash or find food. Thousands of desperate farmers headed west, hoping to find opportunity. Others stood in bread lines organized by charitable organizations.

Hoover resisted calls for federal aid, urging states to step in and help their people. In New York, Governor Roosevelt aggressively took on the challenge of lifting his state out of economic ruin. He asked the legislature to set aside $20 million and used the funds for a public works program and to help the needy.

FDR criticized Hoover for insisting that the federal government leave the responsibility of public relief to charitable organizations, volunteers, and local governments. He felt the federal government and the states had a role. He asked the New York legislature to examine the issue of unemployment insurance and other means of supporting the unemployed. He recommended $20 million be raised in new taxes to start a works program. In his August 28, 1931, message to the legislature, he called on them to do their duty: "Our government is not the master but the creature of the people. The duty of the State toward the citizens is the duty of the servant to its master . . . One of these duties of the State is that of caring for those of its citizens who find themselves the victims of such adverse circumstances as makes them unable to obtain even the necessities for mere existence without the aid of others."

Hoover became a scapegoat for the ills of the Great Depression. His proposals, which might have been sound economic policy during ordinary times, were ineffective. Instead of federal aid, he preached a combination of volunteerism and local government aid. It was a weak response.

In addition, Hoover didn't have the right demeanor for the times. Instead of empathy and leadership, he was defensive. He told people things weren't so bad, when clearly, they were. "No one is actually starving," he said. It was the wrong message during a time of great suffering.

The Republican Party stood with Hoover in the presidential election of 1932. The Democrats turned to FDR. As governor of the nation's most populous state, he had positioned himself to be the voice of the nation. He was the most talked-about prospect for 1932, and in the early days, no other Democrat even came close.

But FDR would soon find out that it would take more than public admiration to get to the White House. He was about to embark upon the toughest campaign of his career.

4

IN THE FOOTSTEPS OF COUSIN TEDDY

WHEN HE WAS FIVE years old, Franklin Roosevelt joined his father at a White House meeting with President Grover Cleveland, a friend of the family. The president bent down to address the boy. "My little man," he said, "I am making a strange wish for you. It is that you may never be president of the United States." No one in the room realized that being president was something FDR would aspire to.

During Hoover's disastrous term, many people wondered if Franklin might follow in his cousin Teddy's footsteps to the White House. FDR's polio didn't end the dream. His physical struggles gave him a seriousness and authority. In his second term as governor of New York, he was far more emotionally and intellectually suited for high office than he had been before he became ill. So, it didn't come as a surprise on January 22, 1932, when FDR announced he would be a candidate for president of the United States.

Eleanor, who hated life in the spotlight, was secretly unhappy with her husband's decision to run for president. But she set aside her personal feelings to support him fully—as she always would.

FDR added James A. Farley, the secretary of the New York State Democratic Committee, to his campaign team. "Big Jim" was tall and burly, with a shiny bald head and a beaming, good-natured personality. He had an instinct for politics and he knew how to win support for FDR in a crowded field that included nine candidates.

Another member of Roosevelt's team—which came to be known as Roosevelt's Brain Trust—was Raymond Moley, a professor of government and public law at Columbia University. Moley wrote some of FDR's speeches, including his remarks about the "forgotten man." A radio program offered each of the candidates ten minutes to speak to the American people. Roosevelt criticized the Hoover administration, arguing that "These unhappy times call for the building of plans . . . that put their faith once more in the forgotten man at the bottom of the economic pyramid."

Hoover said he expected the Depression to be over by Election Day, expressing confidence that he would easily win reelection. Hoover tried to make things difficult for FDR. In April, he invited the nation's governors to dinner at the White House. FDR attended with Eleanor, and like all public occasions, he went through the grueling and painful process of "walking" upright, gripping the arms of aides. When they arrived at the hall, he was exhausted by the exertion and looked forward to sitting down. But Hoover was not yet in the room, and it was expected that everyone remain standing until the president was seated. Roosevelt was sweating, and a White House aide asked if he'd like to take a seat. He refused, gritting his teeth and remaining balanced upright on his crutches for thirty minutes until Hoover arrived. Roosevelt's aides and Eleanor thought Hoover was deliberately late to make FDR look weak. If so, it didn't work.

In the summer of 1932, the Republicans nominated Hoover for another term. "I am deeply grateful for the highest honor that the party can confer," he responded by telegram. "It marks your approval and your confidence." That may not be the only way to look at things: Hoover was chosen with resignation, not inspiration.

The Democratic convention in Chicago was messier. FDR stayed in New York, allowing others to represent him. At the convention, Louis Howe and Farley worked the floor, setting up phone calls with FDR back in Albany so he could make personal appeals to delegates. Delegates endured long hours of speeches in blistering heat. Farley had the foresight to bring a supply of paper fans bearing FDR's image. The hall got so hot that even delegates supporting other candidates gratefully waved them.

The balloting went late into the night. Roosevelt followed the convention on the radio. To distract himself from the stressful ups and downs of the voting, adviser Samuel Rosenman pulled out his notes for Roosevelt's acceptance speech, which had mostly been written by Raymond Moley, but still lacked a soaring ending. Rosenman decided to tackle the ending, eventually scribbling a line on a scrap of paper: "I pledge you, I pledge myself, to a *new deal* for the American people."

When he handed the scrap to Roosevelt, he glanced at the words and nodded. He thought it was "all right," he said, before returning his attention to the radio.

After some backroom negotiations, FDR agreed to

make Speaker of the House John Nance Garner his vice presidential running mate, and his choice assured him votes from Texas and California, as well as support from newspaperman William Randolph Hearst. FDR and Garner were not natural allies. Garner was a fiscal conservative who often sided with Hoover on economic matters. Roosevelt won the nomination.

Normally, the candidate did not accept the nomination at the convention, but held a ceremony weeks later. But Roosevelt announced that he was going to fly to Chicago that day and accept the nomination in person. He felt this would convey a sense of urgency, and also show the nation he was strong and prepared, not a weak, fading cripple.

When he arrived in Chicago where the convention was being held, Howe handed FDR a speech he had written. "You know I can't deliver a speech that I've never done any work on myself, and that I've never even read," Roosevelt said. "It will sound stupid, and it's silly to think that I can."

But after he read Howe's draft, he used a combination of Howe's speech and Moley's. The last paragraphs brought the delegates to their feet in applause.

Out of every crisis, every tribulation, every disaster, mankind rises with some share of greater knowledge, of higher decency, of purer purpose. Today we shall have come through a period of loose thinking and descending morals, an era of selfishness of individual men and women and of whole nations . . . I pledge you, I pledge myself, to a new deal for the American people. Let us all here assembled constitute ourselves prophets of a new order of competence and of courage. This is more than a political campaign. It is a call to arms. Give me your help, not to win votes alone, but to win in this crusade to return America to its own people.

"Happy Days Are Here Again" played as delegates danced in the aisles and FDR grinned and waved. The "new deal" was headlined in major newspapers the next day. By Election Day, it was capitalized—the New Deal.

Just after Hoover accepted his party's nomination for a second term, thousands of angry war veterans stormed down Pennsylvania Avenue to demand relief. They had suffered during World War I, and in 1924, Congress granted them bonuses for their service: $1 a day for service at home (up to $500) and $1.25 a day for service overseas (up to $625). They were given certificates, scheduled to mature in 1945. But they needed the money now, so a group known as the Bonus Army came to Washington to plead with Congress for an advance on their compensation. They set up tents around Washington and vowed to stay until they collected their money.

Legislation to pay the bonuses passed the House of Representatives, but failed in the Senate. The veterans protested, but the Hoover administration was unmoved. By the end of July, Hoover decided the display must end. His attorney general ordered the veterans to go home. When police tried to force them to go, two marchers were killed.

Hoover ordered the army to clear the camps. Six hundred soldiers marched into the streets. Five tanks rolled along, with Secretary of the Army Douglas MacArthur in command. The military leader was now preparing to fire on the men who had served under him in war.

As crowds swarmed in alarm and fear, the military drove the Bonus Army out of the city and set fire to their camps. Hoover tried to defend his action, suggesting the veterans were plants organized by the Communists. Nobody believed the claim because most Americans felt just as desperate as the veterans.

Party advisers urged FDR to limit campaigning to protect his health, but he wouldn't listen. FDR launched a nine-thousand-mile cross-country trip aboard a specially outfitted campaign train. FDR suffered only one physical mishap while campaigning. He was standing and gripping a podium at a rally in Georgia when the podium fell over, toppling Roosevelt into the orchestra pit below. Without missing a beat, his aides dragged him back onto the stage, and he continued speaking. He didn't say anything about the fall, but when he finished, he got a standing ovation from the crowd. Notably, the fall was not reported in the press.

In contrast to Roosevelt's tour across the country, President Hoover preferred a "Rose Garden" campaign strategy, delivering only a handful of speeches. His campaign couldn't be defined by political slogans, and his unpopularity was clear. He could not escape the constant reports about his failures.

On the night of the election, family and friends gathered for a buffet dinner at the Roosevelts' East Sixty-Fifth Street house in New York City before heading over to the National Committee headquarters at the Biltmore Hotel. FDR sat at a large table, with a radio and telephones, and kept score as the night went on. As the returns came in, the news became celebratory.

It was a landslide. FDR carried 42 states, with 472 electoral votes, to Hoover's 6 states and 59 electoral votes. The popular vote margin was vast—22.8 million to 15.7 million votes.

Eleanor was happy for her husband, thinking the victory "would make up for the blow that fate had dealt him when he was stricken with infantile paralysis." But she had mixed feelings; she had enjoyed her independence and knew that she would have very little privacy in the White House.

At the end of the long night, James took his father home and helped him into bed. Before James left, FDR looked up at his son. "You know, Jimmy," he said, "all my life I have been afraid of only one thing—fire. Tonight, I think I'm afraid of something else."

"Afraid of what, Pa?" James asked.

"I'm just afraid that I may not have the strength to do this job," FDR said, in a rare moment of self-doubt. He asked his son to pray for him. "I am going to pray that God will help me, that he will give me the strength and guidance to do this job and to do it right. I hope you will pray for me, too."

In the months between the election and inauguration, FDR worked to put together his cabinet. Given the mess the country was in, few people were rushing to join Roosevelt's White House. One by one, Roosevelt lined up the team he wanted. One of his most progressive picks was Frances Perkins as secretary of labor, the first woman to serve as a cabinet secretary. She had served as commissioner of the Department of Labor in New York State when he was governor, and had been an effective champion of labor issues for over twenty years. She would remain with Roosevelt's administration until the end, making a large contribution, including drafting the Social Security Act.

The Depression worsened as Inauguration Day approached. On February 14, 1933, the Michigan governor announced that the banks would be closed for eight days, trying to halt a run on banks that had swept the nation. The following day, FDR was in Miami to deliver an address to an American Legion gathering. Twenty thousand people crowded into Bayfront Park to listen to Roosevelt, who was accompanied by Chicago mayor Anton Cermak. Roosevelt delivered a short speech, then he sat down.

At that moment, someone fired five shots, hitting Cermak and four bystanders. The target had been FDR, but he was saved, probably due to the quick action of a woman in the crowd. She was standing next to the shooter as he lifted his gun, and she swung her purse and hit him in the arm, shifting his aim just enough for the shots to miss Roosevelt.

The Secret Service rushed Roosevelt away from the scene, but he stopped them when he saw Cermak lying on the ground. FDR ordered him placed in his car, and he cradled Cermak all the way to the hospital. Cermak died a few weeks later; the other victims recovered.

The shooter was an unemployed bricklayer, who told

police he hated everyone who was rich and had intended to kill Roosevelt. The assassin was tried for first-degree murder and received the death penalty. The woman whose quick action had saved the president-elect was invited to FDR's inauguration and attended the inaugural ball.

Three days after the assassination attempt, FDR received a telegram from Hoover on the worsening bank crisis. Hoover urged him to come to the White House to make a joint public statement agreeing to a series of measures to restore public confidence. FDR refused.

Shortly before the inauguration, Hoover again tried, asking FDR to make a joint proclamation calling for a bank holiday. "Like hell I will," FDR said. "If you haven't the guts to do it yourself, I'll wait until I'm president to do it."

Hoover was furious. He felt Roosevelt was playing politics with the life of the nation. FDR did not want Hoover's name attached to any successful effort. In a move that no doubt angered Hoover, Roosevelt announced a bank holiday two days after taking office.

PART TWO

SEEKING GREATNESS

5

PRESIDENT ROOSEVELT

ON FEBRUARY 27, 1933, Franklin Roosevelt sat in front of an evening fire to work on the inauguration address he would deliver the following week. The previous day, Raymond Moley had given FDR a typed draft of the speech for his review, and FDR had spent the day going over it line by line. Now he began to copy the draft in longhand on a legal pad, making edits as he went along. For hours, he rewrote sentences and discussed each phrase with Moley. Once the recopied and edited draft was completed, Moley tossed his typewritten version into the fire.

"This is your speech now," he said.

Indeed, FDR's handwritten copy became the official version. To this day, it remains at the FDR Library in Hyde Park, with a note from Roosevelt attached: "The Inaugural Address as written at Hyde Park on Monday, February 27, 1933. I started in about 9:00 p.m. and ended at 1:30 a.m. A number of minor changes were made in subsequent drafts but the final draft is substantially the same as this original."

Moley, who would grow disillusioned with the Roosevelt administration early on, later defended his authorship of the original, which he'd set alight. He resented the omission of his role in its creation so much that he wrote a second memoir in 1966 to set the record straight. "Some historians accept the note as an indication that on the night of February 27 Roosevelt sat down all alone in his library at Hyde Park and dashed off the draft," he wrote. ". . . The omission of the fact that I was present with him that night, that I had put before him a draft that I had prepared after much consideration and many conferences with him seems strange . . ."

Interestingly, the original handwritten version did not have the speech's most famous words, "The only thing we have to fear is fear itself," in the first paragraph. FDR continued to refine the speech, and when the final version was typed, it included the revised first paragraph:

I am certain that my fellow Americans expect that on my induction into the Presidency I will address them with a candor and a decision which the present situation of our Nation impels. This is preeminently the time to speak the truth, the whole truth, frankly and boldly. Nor need we shrink from honestly facing conditions in our country today. This great Nation will endure as it has endured, will revive and will prosper. So, first of all, let me assert my firm belief that the only thing we have to fear is fear itself—nameless, unreasoning, unjustified terror which paralyzes needed efforts to convert retreat into advance.

It has never been entirely clear where the new first paragraph came from, but speechwriter Samuel Rosenman believed the words to be FDR's own. Millions of Americans heard the speech on their radios, and the line about fear stayed with them. Many decades later, people still consider it a rallying cry for the era. FDR was calling on the nation to be fearless, to rise above their circumstances.

Roosevelt loved speechwriting, speechmaking, and simply speaking, as he did in his fireside chats. His emotionally loaded words were calls to action, to courage, and to renewal. He gave hundreds of speeches, many of them memorable, during his twelve-plus years in office.

Yet he did not have an official speechwriting team in the White House as later presidents did. Instead, he relied on a group of trusted aides and people who knew his thinking and could capture his intention and voice. Chief among these early on were Rosenman and Moley.

Once in the White House, Roosevelt would periodically call together various aides and advisers for speechwriting sessions. He insisted on being closely involved in the process, and when he left the room, the others stayed behind, sometimes long into the night, perfecting the text.

FDR was a careful editor, rereading and reshaping his speeches, adding words and changing the order of paragraphs. The process helped him memorize his remarks so that he could speak more intimately to his audiences.

Roosevelt was sensitive to claims that his speeches were not of his own making. He set the record straight in his official papers: "In preparing a speech I usually take the various drafts and suggestions which have been submitted to me and also the material which has been accumulated in the speech file on various subjects, read them carefully, lay them aside, and then dictate my own draft . . . Naturally, the final speech will contain some of the thoughts and even some of the sentences which appeared in some of the drafts or suggestions submitted."

Understanding that copies of FDR's speeches and

fireside chats were historical documents, his secretary made sure they were returned to her for safekeeping.

On March 3, 1933, the day before the inauguration, the Roosevelts and their son James visited the White House for a traditional social call. They were ushered into the Green Room on the first floor, then made to wait. Mrs. Hoover entered after a few minutes, but there was no sign of the president for half an hour. When Hoover finally arrived, he was joined by an aide. FDR did not want to turn their social call into a policy meeting.

FDR said he would not bring up any serious discussion on a purely social occasion, and in any case, he would want his own advisers present for such a meeting. The rest of the conversation was barely civil.

When the visit finally ended, Roosevelt said, "Mr. President, as you know, it is rather difficult for me to move in a hurry. It takes me a little while to get up, and I know how busy you must be, sir, so please don't wait for me."

Hoover rose and gave Roosevelt a cold look. "Mr. Roosevelt, after you have been president for a while, you will learn that the President of the United States waits for no one." He walked out without another word, leaving his embarrassed wife behind to say her flustered goodbyes. FDR shrugged off the rudeness. He knew what it felt like to lose an election. He also accepted that the president was angry at him for not working with him during the transition.

The next morning, Saturday, March 4, the skies were overcast but the temperature was mild as FDR and his family attended services at Saint John's Episcopal Church across from the White House. Afterward, the president-elect returned to his hotel before leaving for the short trip to the White House's north entrance. He waited for Hoover in the car, which would be followed by one carrying First Lady Lou Hoover and Eleanor.

During the thirty-minute ride to the Capitol, Hoover and FDR sat mostly in silence. FDR tried a couple of times to make conversation and received no response.

Crowds lined the roadway, cheering. Roosevelt glanced at Hoover, who was staring straight ahead, his hands in his lap. FDR thought the crowds deserved acknowledgment—a smile and a wave—but he did not want to overstep if the president made no move. Hoover knew the cheers were not for him, so he refused to do anything. Eventually, FDR removed his top hat and began to wave it in the air to the delight of the well-wishers.

When it was time to take the oath of office, FDR stood. As the Marine band played "Hail to the Chief," he gripped his son's reliable arm and made his way to the podium. After Roosevelt was sworn in, a twenty-one-gun salute rang out. FDR then addressed the crowds and the millions of Americans listening to their radios at home. "The people of the United States have not failed," he said. "In their need they have registered a mandate that they want direct, vigorous action. They have asked for discipline and direction under leadership. They have made me the present instrument of their wishes. In the spirit of the gift I take it."

As the crowd roared, the new president grabbed his son's arm and slowly made his way off the stage. Hoover rose and left. Like every president being replaced, he knew he was no longer the story of the day. "Democracy is not a kind employer," he wrote of his ouster. "The only way out of elective office is to get sick or die or get kicked out." He also felt relief; the fate of the nation was in another man's hands.

The inauguration parade included forty marching bands and representatives from all the states. FDR stayed to watch until the end. When he entered the White House for the first time as president, he found a reception of two thousand people, organized by Eleanor. He slipped past the crowds and went upstairs to the Lincoln Study, for a mass swearing-in of his cabinet.

After dinner, Eleanor left with family members for the inaugural ball, while Roosevelt retired to the Lincoln

Study with his adviser Louis Howe. They sat and talked late into the evening. For twenty-two years they'd been a team, Howe believing in FDR even when Roosevelt did not have faith in himself. Howe was as responsible as anyone for putting FDR in the White House. The two shared a special friendship. Howe would continue to call the president "Franklin," proof of a deep bond that no one could take away.

6

GOVERNING IN CRISIS

PRESIDENT FRANKLIN ROOSEVELT'S PRESS secretary
Stephen Early wanted to establish an open relationship
with the media. Hoover had required reporters to sub-
mit their questions in writing, and then he would choose
which ones to answer. At Early's suggestion, Roosevelt
agreed to answer questions at random, calling on a
range of reporters, rather than just his favorites. FDR
also agreed that press conferences should be frequent
and predictable; Wednesday mornings at 10:00, to meet
the deadlines of the afternoon newspapers, and Friday

afternoons at 4:00 for the weekend and Sunday papers.

FDR held his first press conference on March 8 in the Oval Office. Roosevelt greeted each reporter with a handshake as they crowded into the room. His opening statement took them all by surprise. "I am told that what I am about to do will become impossible, but I am going to try it," he said. "We are not going to have any more written questions and of course while I cannot answer seventy-five or a hundred questions because I simply haven't got the physical time, I see no reason why I should not talk to you ladies and gentlemen off the record just the way I have been doing in Albany and the way I used to do it in the Navy Department down here."

Great news for reporters, but there was a catch. For one thing, he told them, he would not respond to speculation or answer any "if" questions. Follow-up questions—what FDR called "cross-examination"—would not be permitted. In addition, he would sometimes speak off the record, meaning not for direct quotation, during his press conferences. Early often provided reporters with copies of quotes that they could use.

FDR enjoyed talking about his programs. In his first term, he held 337 press conferences. The strict rules about off-the-record comments eventually became loosened, and reporters enjoyed their regular access to the president.

There was little diversity among the reporters. No African American reporters were admitted, theoretically because most black newspapers were weeklies. In spite of Roosevelt addressing the press as "ladies and gentlemen," no women were invited to attend.

Eleanor didn't like the exclusion of women. If a female reporter was excluded from the source of news, she would be less competitive and might even lose her job. In response, Eleanor began holding women-only news conferences. She announced that they would cover issues of importance to the women of the nation. The women's press conferences provided positive coverage for Eleanor, and gave her a public profile she had not had before.

FDR tried to reach out to the American people. To accomplish this, he began holding presidential fireside chats, as a way of having a conversation with the American people on the radio in the intimacy of their living rooms. He held the first chat on March 12 to discuss banking. It began as a tutorial, explaining that much of the money placed in a bank is used for loans so that other people and businesses can borrow it to buy houses and invest in their businesses. He said that the current bank crisis was caused by too many people trying to remove their cash from banks.

"Because of undermined confidence on the part of the public, there was a general rush by a large portion of our population to turn bank deposits into currency or gold—a rush so great that the soundest banks could not get enough currency to meet the demand," Roosevelt said. On March 3, Roosevelt closed the banks. "It was then that I issued the proclamation providing for the nationwide bank holiday, and this was the first step in the Government's reconstruction of our financial and economic fabric."

Americans listened and responded. Roosevelt's chat helped end the rush of people trying to withdraw money from the failing banks. He called Congress into an emergency session, giving them a proposal for the Emergency Banking Relief Act, which allowed the government to reorganize some banks. The measure worked: in the coming weeks, Americans began to redeposit almost $1 billion into the banks.

The New Deal was underway. FDR kept Congress in session for three months as he issued an alphabet soup of legislative initiatives, including the Federal Emergency Relief Act (FERA), which provided assistance to the unemployed through the states; the Agricultural Adjustment Act (AAA), which adjusted farm prices; the Public Works Administration (PWA), which created jobs through building projects; the Glass-Steagall Act, which gave the government supervision of banks; the Securities and Exchange Act, which created the Securities and Exchange Commission (SEC), to help regulate the stock market; the Civilian Conservation Corps (CCC), which put people to work planting trees, restoring forests, and building campgrounds; the National Industrial Recovery Act, which regulated industry on wages and prices; and the Civil Works Administration (CWA), which built national infrastructure. Thanks to Eleanor, those jobs would also be open to women.

The Roosevelts wanted the White House to serve as the people's house. FDR told the staff that any person who called the White House in trouble must be spoken with and helped, if possible. Never before or since had so many guests and workers been invited to live on the premises, either temporarily or permanently. Eleanor thought nothing of inviting guests to stay over.

Eleanor welcomed Henrietta Nesbitt and her husband, down-and-out neighbors from Hyde Park. Nesbitt was put in charge of the kitchen, despite having no experience, and, by all accounts, little talent. The meals prepared at her direction included unappetizing items such as gelatin-filled salads, bread and butter sandwiches, deviled eggs with tomato sauce, and prune whip. State dinners became an embarrassment, private meals a misery. Eleanor, who believed the White House should serve the same frugal meals served by American families, ignored her husband's complaints.

Sara Roosevelt spent most of her time at Hyde Park but remained a regular guest at the White House. She gossiped about her daughter-in-law and complained that Eleanor brought riffraff into the White House. At one point, Sara suggested that the African American domestic staff should be replaced by whites. Eleanor dropped her normal deference to her mother-in-law and said, "I have never told you this before, but I must tell you now. You run your house, and I'll run mine."

Eleanor became an activist First Lady who visited inner-city neighborhoods and farm and mining communities. In her travels, Eleanor insisted on driving her own car, often alone, because she didn't like having the Secret Service around.

The nation seemed to be standing with FDR, and the Democrats won the midterm elections in 1934. By the following year, however, some began to sour on Roosevelt's plans. Both Democrats and Republicans criticized FDR's plan for a social security bill calling for taxes to be withheld throughout workers' lives, with a form of pension issued after retirement. Democrats criticized the idea of taking any money from workers' paychecks; Republicans argued it would create a welfare state.

While the Social Security Act ultimately passed and was signed into law, it was clear Congress was less willing to go along with every one of Roosevelt's programs.

The Supreme Court then began chipping away at parts of the New Deal. The court unanimously ruled that the National Industrial Recovery Act, which set wage and price controls, was unconstitutional. It also ruled against the Agricultural Adjustment Act. FDR was furious.

By 1936—an election year—Roosevelt's popularity seemed to be waning, and he was getting battered by the press. Democrats in Congress wanted to scale back on New Deal programs. Even his own aides were doubting him. When Roosevelt asked Raymond Moley to draft a convention speech, he was appalled at the conservative tone of the remarks. FDR was also experiencing the sting of preparing for an election without Louis Howe by his side; Howe had died in April 1936 after more than six months in the hospital.

Even though he was less popular than he once was, Roosevelt won another landslide victory.

Two weeks after his second inauguration, FDR made one of the biggest mistakes of his presidency: he tried to change the makeup of the Supreme Court. In the early years of his administration, the Supreme Court had supported his New Deal programs. In time, the court began to push back at the constitutionality of his programs, and Congress began to limit its support.

On February 5, 1937, FDR asked Congress to give him the authority to appoint an additional justice for every member of the court over the age of seventy. That could mean up to six additional Supreme Court judges, as well as forty-four judges on the lower federal courts. He argued that his plan would make the courts more efficient. The public was outraged. Most people recognized the plan as an attempt to pack the court before it dismantled more of the New Deal.

In July, Congress defeated the measure, and it never made a reappearance.

During Roosevelt's second term, the nation faced the growing possibility of war in Europe. FDR had been worried about the rise of Adolf Hitler for years, but he and the Congress had maintained a policy of neutrality. The public did not support United States involvement in another foreign war, having sacrificed so much in World War I. During his 1936 presidential campaign, Roosevelt promised that American soldiers would not be sent to fight in foreign wars.

Ironically, Adolf Hitler—the man who would rise to power on a platform of nationalism—was not born in Germany but in neighboring Austria-Hungary. He did not become a German citizen until 1932. When he came to power, he annexed, or took over, the country of his birth, making it part of the Fatherland in 1936.

Hitler's rise to power was unusual. He grew up in a middle-class family—his father was a customs official—and he dropped out of school at age sixteen to become an artist. In 1907, at eighteen, he applied to the Academy of Fine Arts, Vienna, and was rejected. He applied a second time and was turned down again. Devastated, he moved to Munich, where he drew postcards of local sights. His rejection from the artistic community fueled his anti-Semitism; he believed Jews controlled the arts.

After serving in the Bavarian army in World War I, Hitler joined the German Workers' Party. Hitler discovered that he was able to stir crowds and thrill audiences with his speeches. He rose in power, in part because the German people felt great despair after their defeat in the First World War. Within a year, Hitler had seized control of the party, changing its name to the National Socialist German Workers Party, Nazi for short.

The Nazis attacked the government for its failure to restore the economy, which was sinking due to the heavy burden of war payments and the collapsing currency. The German government's weakness enraged Hitler and the Nazis. In 1923, he tried to overthrow the government, which landed him in jail for treason.

Hitler served nine months of a five-year sentence, but during his incarceration he wrote the first volume of *Mein Kampf*, translated as "My Struggle." It argued the superiority of the Aryan race—"true Germans"—over other races, especially Jews. He wrote that the Nazi Party was "obligated to promote the victory of the better and stronger, and demand the subordination of the inferior and weaker in accordance with the eternal will that dominates this universe." This became the justification for everything he did after that. It was a slow process, but by the time the stock market crashed in 1929, the Nazis were ready to take over.

At first, it seemed that the Nazi Party would remain a loud but ineffective resistance party. As the economy worsened, the party gained followers. In the national election of 1930, the Nazis become the second largest political party in the nation. In 1932, the same year FDR won the presidency, Hitler ran against the elderly German president Paul von Hindenburg. He didn't win, but he denied Hindenburg the majority he needed to govern. The government was in chaos, so Hindenburg appointed Hitler chancellor.

Within weeks, Hitler seized control of power. By March 1933, he forced Hindenburg to give him absolute "emergency" authority. Soon after taking power, Hitler began trying to restore Germany's glory. He immediately began limiting Jewish freedoms and organizing a brutal law-enforcement body, the Gestapo, to carry out his will. When Hindenburg died, Hitler announced that he would assume power, not as president but as führer, supreme leader.

He had a two-part plan. First, he planned to conquer other nations to increase German territory. Second, he planned to eliminate the Jewish people. He was deadly serious about both goals.

As the world watched with growing concern, there was little official resistance to Hitler. In England, the attitude was wait and see. Only one voice stood out— that of Winston Churchill, a conservative member of the House of Commons, who had been railing against Hitler since he became chancellor.

On November 5, 1937, Hitler held a secret conference in Berlin where he outlined his program. By that point, he was unstoppable.

British prime minister Neville Chamberlain approached Hitler with the proposition that they were two reasonable men, both seeking to avoid war, and spoke of discussions held in a spirit of collaboration and goodwill. He thought Nazism could be contained.

With this purpose in mind, Chamberlain convinced Hitler to hold a high-level meeting in Munich in September 1938 to bring together Germany, France, Great Britain, and Italy and reach an agreement that would keep the peace. The issue on the table was Hitler's desire to annex a region of Czechoslovakia heavily populated by ethnic Germans. Czechoslovakia had no representation at the conference. The idea of one nation taking over another, without any provocation, in order to further its own power, was a terrible breach of civilized conduct. However, with Italy's Benito Mussolini on Hitler's side, Chamberlain and French prime minister Édouard Daladier gave in, thinking this small gesture would prevent all-out war. The Munich Pact allowed Hitler to take over the Sudetenland region of Czechoslovakia without resistance from their two countries.

In Great Britain, Churchill was alarmed by the Munich Pact. His concern would eventually reach President Roosevelt in Washington. For the first five years of FDR's presidency, he acted independently; he was the sole director of his policies. That would change when war would force him to work collaboratively with other world leaders, including Winston Churchill.

7

FRANKLIN AND WINSTON

IN 1938, THE BRITISH considered Winston Churchill a
has-been. At sixty-four, he had a seat in the House of
Commons, the lower house of Parliament, but he had
little power. What he did have was the conviction that
Adolf Hitler needed to be stopped.

After the Munich Pact was signed, Churchill knew
that many British citizens were relieved that war had
been avoided. But Churchill believed that appeasing
Hitler was not the road to peace. Churchill was right:
the following year, Hitler would break the pact, invad-
ing all of Czechoslovakia.

Churchill's initial response to the Munich Pact was a fiery speech in Parliament, followed by a radio address to the people of the United States, making clear, as he would do many times, that Hitler posed a global threat. "Far away, happily protected by the Atlantic and Pacific Oceans, you, the people of the United States . . . are the spectators . . . of these tragedies and crimes," Churchill said. "We are left in no doubt where American conviction and sympathies lie; but will you wait until British freedom and independence have succumbed, and then take up the cause when it is three-quarters ruined, yourselves alone?"

Like President Franklin Roosevelt, Churchill was flawed. He could be stubborn and emotional, high-spirited and subject to dark moods and an explosive temper. He was a heavy smoker and drinker. He didn't walk; he stomped, spearing the ground with his walking stick. Many of his peers thought that he should think about retirement, but Churchill barreled on.

He set his sights on FDR, trying to convince him to join the fight against Hitler. The two men were not natural collaborators in the beginning. FDR preferred a less strident approach to world affairs. But eventually they would come to realize how much they needed each other.

Churchill understood that Americans were not eager

to join another war. The United States was not fully out of the Depression, but, helped by the New Deal, the economy was starting to stabilize. FDR still considered the threat posed by Hitler as something that could be managed and negotiated. In September, shortly before the Munich Pact was signed, FDR had sent a telegram to Hitler, urging him to find a way to peacefully negotiate with Czechoslovakia. In his response, Hitler said that he was a man of peace being threatened and treated unfairly.

FDR thought that Hitler could be pressured into compliance. Congress had passed neutrality laws in the mid-1930s, directing the United States to stay on the sidelines of any foreign war. On April 14, 1939, FDR sent a seven-page telegram to Hitler and Italian prime minister Benito Mussolini, who had allied himself with Hitler, urging them not to invade any other European countries. This time Hitler didn't bother to respond. Instead, he mocked the president's words at a speech before the German government, basically telling the president not to meddle in the affairs of foreign governments, which had their own priorities.

Hitler's treatment of the Jews became alarming. Jews had been suffering under the Nazis for years, but the world had mostly ignored the issue until November 9, 1938. In retaliation for the assassination of a

German diplomat in Paris by a Jewish teenager of Polish descent, Nazis rioted across Germany, Austria, and part of Czechoslovakia. They destroyed synagogues, smashed and burned Jewish stores, and assaulted Jews in the streets. The Nazis ordered police and firefighters to stand by and do nothing. More than seven thousand Jewish businesses, homes, and schools were destroyed and nearly one hundred Jews were murdered. Blaming the Jews for the riots, authorities arrested 30,000 Jewish men and sent them to concentration camps. The event became known as Kristallnacht, "The Night of Broken Glass."

Jews were desperate to leave Nazi-controlled areas, and at first Hitler was willing to let them go. The United States and other nations were asked to help the Jewish refugees, but Roosevelt didn't grasp the scope of the problem, and thousands of refugees were turned away. Later, when the full details of Nazi atrocities were revealed, FDR was criticized for not acting earlier, when it might have made a bigger difference. In retrospect, FDR's record on helping the Jews would be mixed.

FDR was making a calculated bet. He didn't think Americans would fight a war to save the Jews. Roosevelt failed to say much publicly about the plight of the Jews, fearing he would lose the support he had for the war effort.

Some people, including Joseph Kennedy, United States ambassador to Great Britain, blamed the Jews for the conflict. Worse was pilot Charles Lindbergh, whose solo flight across the Atlantic in 1927 had made him an American hero. He was an isolationist with pro-Nazi sympathies; he insisted Nazism was not a threat to America.

FDR thought war in Europe was inevitable. As he tried to determine America's course, he turned to Harry Hopkins, who took Louis Howe's place as FDR's closest and most trusted aide. Samuel Rosenman called him "the new Howe." Hopkins became so indispensable that FDR would move him and his family into the White House in 1940.

Crowds cheered as they welcomed King George VI and Queen Elizabeth of England to Washington, DC, in June 1939. The idea of the visit, the first of its kind by British monarchs, had been in the works for months. FDR invited the royal couple to the United States after learning they would be visiting Canada. In a letter to the king on September 17, 1938, FDR wrote, "I think it would be an excellent thing for Anglo-American relations if you could visit the United States . . . It occurs to me that a Canadian trip would be crowded with formalities and that you both might like three or four days of very simple country life at Hyde Park, with no formal entertainments and an opportunity to get a bit of rest and relaxation."

Roosevelt wanted to show his support of the king, whose nation seemed on the brink of war, even if he was bound to remain neutral. Although the visit was social, behind the scenes Roosevelt and the king held important discussions about naval strategies and wartime support.

FDR also wanted to provide the royal couple with a taste of American pleasures, so he invited them to Hyde Park for an all-American picnic. Roosevelt served hot dogs and beer, a menu that scandalized many people, including FDR's mother. Sitting on the porch, the king and queen were eager to try hot dogs for the first time. The monarchs were served their hot dogs on a silver tray, but ate them on paper plates.

The royal visit had a sobering impact on the Roosevelts. Now the king and queen were like friends. Meeting the royals brought the fear felt in Britain home and made it real. War was a looming threat, but not yet a reality. England was desperate for allies. On August 23, 1939, England received a blow when Germany and the Soviet Union signed a nonaggression pact, an agreement that further isolated England. Nonaggression was not the same as an alliance; it meant that Stalin would not fight against Hitler, not that he would join Hitler's fight. For the moment, the Soviet Union agreed to remain neutral.

Joseph Stalin, who had exercised absolute power over the Soviet Union since his rise in 1924, was a mystery to the West. Stalin was a child of poverty; his father was a cobbler, given to drunken violence. He was the third born, but both of his older brothers died in infancy, so he was raised as an only child. Stalin's childhood was brutal; his father eventually abandoned the family. Stalin became obsessed with the vision of Karl Marx for a revolution against the monarchy.

He was born Iosif Vissarionovich Dzhugashvili, but he changed his name to Stalin—meaning *man of steel*— as a young man. Stalin became powerful and ruled with force. Capitalist practices were forbidden in favor of collectivization. A deadly famine in 1932 and 1933 that killed an estimated five million people, most of them in Ukraine, was a direct outgrowth of collectivization. But unrest was crushed. Disloyalty to the state—meaning Stalin—was punishable by death. Nearly one million people were murdered in the Great Purge between 1936 and 1938. Millions more were killed or sent to labor camps during his reign.

After signing the nonaggression pact with the Soviets, Hitler showed his hand. On September 1, 1939, a million and a half German troops invaded Poland. Having annexed Austria and Czechoslovakia with almost no response from other nations, Hitler may not have expected much reactions from other countries. This time he had overreached. The day after the invasion, Britain and France told Hitler that he must withdraw from Poland by September 3 or face grave consequences. Hitler ignored the notice. On September 3, Britain and France declared war on Germany.

FDR shared the news with the American people in a fireside chat. "When peace has been broken anywhere, the peace of all countries everywhere is in danger," he said. "This nation will remain a neutral nation, but . . . even a neutral cannot be asked to close his mind or close his conscience."

After war was declared, Churchill was named lord of the admiralty, Britain's version of secretary of the navy, a position Churchill had held during World War I. FDR asked Churchill to keep him informed, and over the course of the war they exchanged nearly two thousand letters.

The American isolationists held fast. On October 13, Lindbergh gave a racially charged speech, saying: "Our bond with Europe is a bond of race and not of political ideology . . . It is the European race we must preserve . . . If the white race is ever seriously threatened, it may then be time for us to take our part in its protection."

FDR would later tell one of his advisers, "I am absolutely convinced that Lindbergh is a Nazi."

America's neutrality was based on laws establishing an embargo against selling arms to states involved in war. On September 21, FDR appeared before Congress to urge them to repeal the arms embargo. He wanted to reset the debate, to frame the issue as a return to American principles. He believed the Neutrality Acts of the 1930s, designed to limit US involvement in foreign wars, damaged American interests by sidelining the nation in a time of true crisis. He presented his proposal not as a step toward engagement in war, but as a safeguard against the looming dangers.

Congress responded, freeing the United States to sell weapons and material to Britain. Critics charged that supplying goods to Britain would compromise America's military readiness. But Roosevelt thought by lending aid in this way, the United States would be able to stay out of the war.

At the time, the American military was not fighting fit. For years during the Depression, military spending had been on the back burner, and it showed. The current military was only a hundred thousand strong—a steep decline from the sixteen million who had served in World War I—and the nation was far behind on weaponry, air and sea vessels, and materials, especially when compared with the strength of the German army. It was cause for alarm.

In September, FDR began to reverse that decline. He appointed General George C. Marshall as army chief of staff, Henry Stimson as secretary of war, and William Franklin Knox as secretary of the navy. Major General Edwin Watson remained FDR's senior military aide. These leaders went to work to prepare the American military machine for whatever threat came its way.

No American president had ever served more than two terms in office. None had even tried, with the exception of Theodore Roosevelt, who ran an independent party campaign after he'd left office. Before 1951, when the Twenty-Second Amendment was ratified, there was no term limit. But ever since President Washington chose to step down after two terms, it was considered the unwritten rule of politics. As the 1940 election approached, many people wondered if FDR was going to break with tradition.

Roosevelt initially planned to retire and write his autobiography. Eleanor didn't want her husband to run again. She felt that he had done his part, and it was time to let the New Deal continue without him. The rest of the family agreed.

But the war in Europe was getting worse. In April,

Nazis invaded Denmark and Norway. On May 10, in a "blitzkrieg"—a lightning attack—German forces flooded into Belgium and Holland, overwhelming their defenses and bombing airfields in Belgium, Holland, France, and Luxembourg.

FDR sat in his office late into the night, reviewing reports from Europe, which were increasingly grim. Prime Minister Chamberlain had resigned. Churchill's position as lord of the admiralty had restored his reputation, and he was ready to serve. Churchill became prime minister.

In the coming weeks, German troops stormed into France. On June 14, Nazi troops marched into Paris, taking the city. Five days later, Churchill sent a message to FDR. "As you are no doubt aware, the scene has darkened swiftly . . . If necessary, we shall continue the war alone, and we are not afraid of that." But he warned Roosevelt that if the United States did not lend its voice and support, before too long it would be too late to have any impact.

The American people opposed joining the war, not wanting to send soldiers to fight, but many thought the United States should help in some way. France was under assault. The idea that Britain might fall to the Nazis was unthinkable.

On June 10, Italy entered the war, aligned with Germany. FDR admired England's resolve, but the effort seemed futile. At the same time, FDR needed to decide about a third term. He felt obligated to continue in office and see the crisis through, but his opponents argued, "Washington wouldn't, Grant couldn't, Roosevelt shouldn't." Even his own vice president, John Nance Garner, opposed a third term and talked about running himself.

The Republicans nominated Wendell Willkie, a successful business executive. Originally a Democrat and supporter of the New Deal, Willkie had changed his mind and his party over what he considered unfair burdens on business.

FDR still hadn't made up his mind about running. He said he had no wish to be nominated; if the delegates wanted him, they would have to draft him. At the Democratic convention, the delegates began to cheer, "We want Roosevelt! We want Roosevelt!" The following day, Roosevelt was nominated with the support of most of the convention.

FDR had always loved campaigning, but in 1940 he was barely on the campaign trail because he had too much to do in Washington. The central issue of the election was not domestic policy but the international crisis. Republicans believed a vote for Roosevelt was a vote for war, and a vote for Willkie was a vote against war.

The news from England was demoralizing. In September, the Germans launched bombing raids on London and other cities. This wasn't an invasion in Germany's typical manner, but a campaign to terrorize the English and weaken their resolve. Night after night bombs fell in a blitz that would continue well into 1941. Churchill was often on the streets, offering words of comfort. The king and queen frequently visited bombed neighborhoods. Buckingham Palace was also bombed; they were all in it together.

At the end of September, Hitler strengthened his hand by formalizing a Tripartite Pact with Italy and Japan. The Axis Powers, as they became known, agreed to divide their efforts, with Germany and Italy leading the fight in Europe and Japan focusing on the Pacific. From FDR's point of view, Japan was the greatest threat to American interests because of its desire to expand control in the Pacific regions. In 1939, FDR had moved the Pacific fleet from California to Pearl Harbor, Hawaii, a United States territory, in an attempt to halt Japanese expansion. The Axis Tripartite Pact promised assistance from the others if one of the parties was attacked by a nation not involved in the war. In other words, if America attacked Japanese ships, it would be the same as declaring war on Germany and Italy.

FDR was frustrated about waiting on the sidelines.

He feared that American involvement in the war was almost certain, but he didn't say that in his campaign. On Election Day, Roosevelt was ahead in the polls but not by much. By late evening it appeared that Roosevelt had won again. The final count was tighter than his previous elections, but still decisive.

Roosevelt knew he had to choose his words carefully. Each fireside chat and speech to Congress was a minefield. He needed to keep the nation unified. One of the speeches that characterized FDR's defense of democracy was the State of the Union address, which became known as the "Four Freedoms" speech.

After working over a number of drafts, FDR said he had an idea for an uplifting ending. After a long pause, he leaned forward in his chair and dictated the text of the Four Freedoms: "We must look forward to a world based on four essential human freedoms," he said, naming them as freedom of speech and expression; freedom to worship God, each in their own way; freedom from want; and freedom from fear. The speech became a standard of American values, repeated down through the decades.

The inauguration on January 20 felt somewhat understated. The nation was adjusting to a third-term president. Republicans were demoralized, having also failed to win majorities in the House and Senate. After the ceremony, the president sat at the parade reviewing stand as General George Marshall led a large group of soldiers down Pennsylvania Avenue, followed by tanks. Air fighters and bombers thundered across the sky above.

Roosevelt's address, which was broadcast throughout the world, recalled the words of George Washington in his first inaugural address in 1789. FDR called on the American people to preserve the "sacred fire of liberty," noting that "if we let it be smothered with doubt and fear—then we shall reject the destiny which Washington strove so valiantly and so triumphantly to establish."

8

THE RISE OF THE ALLIES

ON INAUGURATION DAY, JANUARY 20, 1941, President Franklin Roosevelt wrote a letter of support to British prime minister Winston Churchill, quoting a verse from Henry Wadsworth Longfellow's poem "The Building of the Ship":

> *Sail on, O Ship of State!*
> *Sail on, O Union, strong and great.*
> *Humanity with all its fears*
> *With all the hope of future years,*
> *Is hanging breathless on thy fate!*

Churchill was so moved by the message that he quoted it in a February broadcast, directly addressing the United States: "Put your confidence in us. Give us your faith and your blessing, and under Providence all will be well. We shall not fail or falter; we shall not weaken or tire. Neither the sudden shock of battle nor the long-drawn trials of vigilance and exertion will wear us down. Give us the tools and we will finish the job."

To support Great Britain, FDR pushed for a program known as Lend-Lease. It gave military aid to Britain with the agreement that the materials would be returned at the end of the war. "Suppose my neighbor's home catches fire, and I have a length of garden hose four or five hundred feet away," FDR said in a press conference. "If he can take my garden hose and connect it up with his hydrant, I may help him to put out his fire." He used the example as an argument for lending America's neighbors the materials they needed to fight Adolf Hitler.

The Lend-Lease Act was hotly debated in Congress. Even if America didn't enter the war directly, it became clear that we could no longer refuse to help. The Lend-Lease Act was passed by a bipartisan coalition and signed into law on March 11.

On June 22, Hitler made his boldest move yet, breaking the nonaggression pact and attacking the Soviet Union. He thought Russia was ripe for the picking, telling his generals, "We have only to kick in the door and the whole rotten structure will come crashing down." Hitler believed America would eventually enter the war, and he wanted to invade before an alliance could form between England, the United States, and the Soviet Union. He expected to be able to conquer the Soviet Union in a matter of months.

In the surprise attack, more than three million soldiers and thousands of tanks and aircraft crossed into the Soviet Union. The Russian army was overwhelmed and the air force virtually destroyed.

At first, the Soviets were ill-equipped to fight back. When Nikita Khrushchev, the head of the party in Ukraine, asked the chief of arms production for rifles, he was told that all the rifles had been shipped to Stalingrad.

"Then, what are we supposed to fight with?" Khrushchev asked.

"I don't know," the arms coordinator said. "Pikes, swords, homemade weapons, anything you can make in your own factories."

Khrushchev was stunned. "You mean we should fight tanks with spears?"

"You'll have to do the best you can."

Churchill couldn't imagine the Soviet Union falling to the Nazis. That would make winning the war nearly impossible. "No one has been a more consistent opponent of Communism than I have," he said. "I will unsay no word that I have spoken about it. But all this fades away before the spectacle which is now unfolding." Churchill despised the Soviet regime, but he despised Hitler even more.

Roosevelt was cautious. Now that the Soviet Union was on the side of Great Britain, he realized that its defeat would cripple the fight against Hitler. He sent Harry Hopkins to Moscow to meet with Stalin. There was no reason Lend-Lease would not apply to the Soviets. Americans might balk at sending military aid to the Red Army, but Hitler's attack had made allies of old enemies. By the end of October, $100 billion in shipments were making their way to Russia.

On August 3, FDR left for a fishing trip on Cape Cod. At least, that was what most people, including his wife, believed. But the fishing trip was a carefully staged trick to hide a secret meeting with Churchill. A Secret Service agent dressed like Roosevelt and posed as if he were fishing, while the president slipped away to a secret meeting in Newfoundland.

Churchill left England in secret, too. The two leaders met aboard the USS *Augusta*, surrounded by naval destroyers. To Churchill's disappointment, during the meeting FDR stopped short of pledging commitment to the war. Instead they came up with a statement of common principles, which became known as the Atlantic Charter. Loosely stated, the principles expressed the sovereign rights of self-governance to all people, as well as equal rights to trade, a vow to collaborate openly with all nations, peace on the seas, and a hope, after the defeat of Hitler, that all nations would abandon the use of force. The charter wasn't a formal agreement, and it didn't have an immediate impact on the relationship between the two countries. However, although they didn't know it at the time, the document became the starting framework of a postwar world.

On September 6, FDR returned to Hyde Park because his eighty-six-year-old mother was gravely ill. Roosevelt sat by her bed all day and night, sometimes joined by Eleanor. Sara Roosevelt died quietly just after noon the next day. Shortly after her death, one of the property's most majestic oaks toppled to the ground. FDR returned to Washington with a heavy heart to continue the business of government.

FDR turned his attention to Japan. FDR had long been opposed to Japan's aggressive moves in the East, particularly toward Indochina (modern-day Vietnam and the surrounding areas). When Japan took control of airfields in Indochina, FDR froze Japan's assets in the United States and ordered an embargo on oil and gasoline sales. Japanese ambassador Kichisaburo Nomura was in Washington, trying to make a deal to lift the embargo. The Japanese wanted the United States to stay out of its affairs in Indochina and to restore normal commercial relations. The United States wanted Japan's promise to withdraw from Indochina and end its aggressive stance in the Pacific. America also wanted to encourage Japan to leave the Tripartite Pact with Germany and Italy. At the time, Americans believed Nomura wanted to find a peaceful resolution to the conflicts in the world.

Keeping peace became more difficult in October, when the Japanese prime minister was ousted and was replaced by a more militaristic leader. Saburo Kurusu, a hardliner, was sent by the government to work with Nomura, but the Americans did not trust him. When Nomura and Kurusu tried to rush the Americans into an agreement favorable to the Japanese, FDR resisted.

Additional efforts were made to negotiate a solution, but they got nowhere.

On December 6, Roosevelt tried to avoid conflict by making a direct appeal to Japanese emperor Hirohito. "I address myself to Your Majesty at this moment in the fervent hope that Your Majesty may, as I am doing, give thought in this definite emergency to ways of dispelling the dark clouds," FDR wrote. "I am confident that both of us, for the sake of the peoples not only of our own great countries but for the sake of humanity in neighboring territories, have a sacred duty to restore traditional amity and prevent further death and destruction in the world."

FDR hoped a final appeal from one peace-loving leader to another would make a difference. But the message would never reach Hirohito. It was still in transit to Japan on December 7, 1941, when the United States learned that the Japanese emperor wasn't so peace-loving after all.

9

THE COMMON CAUSE

ON SUNDAY, DECEMBER 7, 1941, at 1:40 p.m., President Franklin Roosevelt learned that Pearl Harbor had been bombed by the Japanese. After confirming the attack, the White House released a statement to the press: "At 7:55 a.m. Hawaiian time, the Japanese bombed Pearl Harbor. The attacks are continuing . . ." By the time of the announcement, the bombing was almost over.

The attack began at 7:55 a.m. Hawaii time (12:55 p.m. in Washington), but the warning signs had appeared earlier. Two privates were manning a radar center north of Oahu, getting ready to go off duty when they noticed what appeared to be a group of incoming planes. They notified the Information Center, and they were told not to worry about it. They closed down the station and went to breakfast.

Moments later, the planes were overhead. Loudspeakers blared: "All hands man your battle stations!" One by one, the battleships were blasted. As the ships burned, survivors plunged overboard, but massive fuel spills had set the water on fire, and they burned alive in the water.

Within two hours, the attack was over, leaving 2,335 dead and 1,143 wounded. The Pacific fleet in Hawaii was nearly lost.

FDR called his cabinet together, and the press gathered outside. As soon as British prime minister Winston Churchill heard the news, he said he wanted to declare war on Japan. After receiving confirmation of the attack from Roosevelt, Churchill said he was going to ask the House of Commons for a declaration of war against Japan the next day.

Churchill was relieved that the United States would now be forced into the war. But he also worried that an American war with Japan might limit Lend-Lease materials, meaning he could have less support, not more, from the United States.

Throughout the evening, FDR met with the cabinet and military leaders. He said the nation faced its gravest moment since Lincoln had announced a civil war in 1861. He said there was no choice but to declare war—indeed, with its attack, Japan had already declared war on the United States.

FDR's son James helped him into bed late that night. He lingered to speak privately to his father. James, who was a captain in the Marine Corps reserve, wanted to serve overseas. He insisted on a combat post, even though he had health problems. FDR did not try to talk him out of it. He knew, with sadness and a degree of pride, that all his sons would want to fight. He recalled his own disappointment at being denied the opportunity to fight during World War I.

During the war, all of FDR's sons served: James fought in the Pacific theater; Elliott became a pilot and flew more than three hundred combat missions; Franklin Jr. became commander of a destroyer in the Pacific; and John, who had joined the navy in early 1941, also served in the Pacific. Their father would now be their commander in chief.

The day after the attack, Roosevelt addressed Congress, saying:

Yesterday, December 7, 1941—a date which will live in infamy—the United States of America was suddenly and deliberately attacked by naval and air forces of the Empire of Japan . . . The attack yesterday on the

Hawaiian Islands has caused severe damage to American naval and military forces. I regret to tell you that very many American lives have been lost. In addition, American ships have been reported torpedoed on the high seas . . . I believe that I interpret the will of the Congress and of the people when I assert that we will not only defend ourselves to the uttermost, but will make it very certain that this form of treachery shall never again endanger us.

The president closed by asking Congress to declare war on Japan.

The House of Representatives and the Senate approved the declaration in an almost unanimous vote. The only "no" vote came from Montana Republican Jeannette Rankin, the first woman to serve in Congress. She was a lifelong pacifist, who had also opposed America's entry into World War I.

On December 11, Germany and Italy declared war on the United States, leading to an American declaration of war with Germany and Italy. This time the vote in Congress was unanimous because Rankin voted "present" instead of "no." She was so unpopular after the vote that she chose not to run for reelection.

Now that the United States was in the war, Churchill wanted to iron out the issues of command and strategy with the president. He arrived in Washington, DC, on December 22, and stayed at the White House. At dinner that night, FDR raised a glass to honor his guest: "I have a toast to offer; it has been in my head and on my heart for a long time. Now it is on the tip of my tongue: to the Common Cause!"

Churchill would remain at the White House until January 14, except for a brief trip to Canada to address Parliament. The Roosevelts attempted to celebrate a normal Christmas with their guest. Christmas Day began with a church service, followed by a lavish feast, including roast turkey with dressing and gravy, beans, cauliflower, a sweet potato casserole, cranberry jelly, a grapefruit salad, and rolls. For dessert, they had plum pudding with hard sauce and ice cream.

Churchill addressed a joint session of Congress the following day. He spoke for thirty minutes about the evils of Japan, and the speech ended with thunderous applause as Churchill gestured with a V for victory. That evening Churchill suffered what might have been a heart attack; doctors ordered six weeks of bed rest. He ignored them and went on.

General Dwight D. Eisenhower did not show his temper often, but the chaos of the war department in Washington during the early days of the war frustrated him. To make matters worse, he wanted to serve at the front, but he was called to Washington to work as a strategic planner under the command of General George C. Marshall. Eisenhower admired Marshall more than any other general, but he felt sidelined in a desk job.

Marshall had to structure a massive military force to defeat Hitler in the West and the Japanese in the Pacific and East Asia. FDR and Churchill held strong opinions, so Marshall had to work to hold on to his independent views. In meetings, Marshall was reserved and dignified; he avoided informal chatter that could lead to agreements he wasn't ready to make.

When necessary, Marshall had no trouble standing up to Roosevelt. He first did so at a meeting in 1938, when he was appointed army chief of staff. FDR pushed for a plan, and everyone in the room agreed with the president, until he asked Marshall.

"Don't you think so, George?" the president asked.

"I am sorry, Mr. President, but I don't agree with you at all," Marshall said, leaving Roosevelt briefly speechless. FDR liked to have his way, as did Churchill, but both men recognized how much they needed a man like Marshall.

Most Americans expected the nation to jump into the fight, but the war department took time to reorganize itself. Meanwhile, Japan was continuing to expand its control of the Pacific, including major attacks on Bataan and Singapore in Indonesia. US citizens were frightened in February when a submarine appeared off the coast of California and fired at the coast. The prospect of direct attacks to our shores was alarming to a nation still numb from Pearl Harbor.

People demanded protection, and they targeted the Japanese Americans living on the West Coast. Rumors and suspicions spread about the possibility that these Americans were loyal to the Japanese cause. In response to public hysteria, congressmen from western states were calling for government action. Secretary of War Henry Stimson met with FDR and proposed a solution that would be unthinkable in ordinary times—relocating Japanese Americans to internment camps for the duration of the war. On February 19, 1942, FDR signed an executive order removing 120,000 Japanese Americans from their homes in "military exclusion zones" on the West Coast and taking them to inland internment camps, their civil rights suspended. Overnight, ordinary families were uprooted from their homes and businesses and sent to hastily built camps where they would live out the war. There was no consideration for their US citizenship or their patriotism. It was just assumed they would take Japan's side.

The internment of Japanese Americans would be a

permanent stain on FDR's war record. It seems unlikely that FDR thought these citizens posed a real threat; if so, why not intern German or Italian Americans as well? More likely, with opinion polls showing 93 percent of Americans supporting internment, it was a political calculation.

In the winter of 1942, the public mood was bitter and scared. FDR gave a fireside chat about the war. He asked newspapers to print maps of the world. He told his aides, "I am going to ask the American people to take out their maps. I'm going to speak about strange places that many of them have never heard of—places that are now the battleground for civilization . . ." He explained that America wasn't an isolated nation, needing only to protect its own shores. The war required a global strategy and effort. He urged Americans to be patient and resolute.

Behind the scenes, the Allies had different approaches and purposes. Stalin wasn't considered a trustworthy ally; he operated on his own, with the aid but not the influence of the Allies. FDR and Churchill worried that Stalin might at some point give in and form an alliance with Germany to save what was left of his country. FDR was also troubled that Great Britain had its own empire to protect, fighting for freedom while protecting colonialism. For example, FDR's open support for India's independence didn't sit well with Churchill, and many Indians were so determined to end British rule that they supported Germany and Japan. FDR wanted to create a postwar world where every nation would be independent, but first they had to win the war.

William Standley, a retired admiral of the US Navy and a longtime friend of FDR, was appointed the new ambassador to the Soviet Union. When he arrived in Moscow, he learned that being ambassador in this secretive country didn't mean having access to information. From the start, he had problems learning critical plans, even from his own government. He was often the last person to know what was going on.

He had almost no contact with ordinary Russians. Conditions were harsh; the entire nation was under strict food rationing. Even the embassy staff had to scrape for food, although they were in far better shape than the locals. The embassy staff also kept chickens on the grounds for eggs and occasional meat.

For Standley's first meeting with Stalin, twelve days after his arrival, he was shown into a conference room with a large, gleaming table. Stalin was seated at one end. Standley's initial impression was that Stalin didn't take the meeting too seriously because he doodled throughout their conversation. After Standley offered the president's greeting, Stalin asked why he was having difficulty receiving Lend-Lease supplies. Standley explained that the ships were often torpedoed and the shipments lost, but he promised to try to improve the situation.

In late May, Stalin sent Vyacheslav Molotov, his foreign minister, to Washington. Molotov was an old Stalin ally from the early days of the Bolshevik Revolution, and he'd been a brutal leader during the Great Purge, ordering the deaths of hundreds of citizens deemed disloyal. Now he was the second most powerful man in the Soviet Union.

His arrival in Washington was shrouded in secrecy; Molotov traveled using the false name "Mr. Brown." He stayed at the White House, in the same room where Churchill had stayed after Pearl Harbor. Eleanor recalled that when a valet had unpacked his bags, he had found a sausage, a loaf of black bread, and a loaded pistol. "The Secret Service men did not like visitors with pistols," she wrote in a rare burst of humor, "but on this occasion nothing was said. Mr. Molotov evidently thought he might have to defend himself and also he might be hungry."

The situation in Russia was desperate, and fearing Russia's collapse, FDR wanted to welcome Molotov to keep the alliance strong. In addition to continuing to ship materials to Russia, Molotov wanted Roosevelt to agree to opening a second front in Western Europe with a cross-Channel invasion of France during 1942, which would pull Nazi troops and resources away from Russia.

Roosevelt considered the action, but Marshall wasn't too sure. For one thing, an assault on France would be high-risk and would take months to orchestrate. Also, Churchill didn't support a cross-Channel invasion of France. Roosevelt was so eager to accommodate Molotov that he urged Marshall to agree to a second front, staying vague about the details and timeline. Molotov left Washington with the promise of opening a second front.

Churchill was enraged. He considered a cross-Channel invasion in 1942 suicidal. His military advisers warned that they didn't have the landing craft to launch the full-scale attack that would be needed. If the effort failed, it could be a fatal blow to Allied interests and would make Hitler even stronger in Europe. It would also be the end of Churchill as prime minister.

Instead, Churchill favored a joint British-American invasion of French North Africa. On June 17, he went to the United States to make his case in person.

Roosevelt had recently scored a major victory against the Japanese at Midway, two critically positioned islands in the middle of the Pacific. After a fierce two-day battle, the Japanese were forced to retreat. The victory destroyed four Japanese carriers and more than 300 aircraft, killed 3,500 Japanese soldiers, and halted Japan's march through the Pacific. It would be considered one of the most decisive battles in the war.

For a second time, Churchill visited FDR in Washington. While meeting with Churchill in the Oval Office, FDR received a note with devastating news for the Allies: Tobruk had fallen. Tobruk was a vital port city in eastern Libya that had been the centerpiece of Middle East strategy since 1940. The city was a gateway to Egypt and the Suez Canal. The prime minister slumped in his chair; he considered this one of the heaviest blows of the war.

"What can we do to help?" Roosevelt asked. Churchill asked FDR to send as many Sherman tanks as he could spare to the Middle East. There was no question about not responding. Although Roosevelt knew he'd take some flak at home for making such a large investment in the Middle East, he also realized he needed to do this for his friend and partner.

The defeat confirmed Churchill's view that a North Africa invasion should be launched as soon as possible. An Allied victory in North Africa would stop Hitler's progress and give the Allies an opening to continue on to Italy and into Europe. It would also provide some relief to Russia. By the end of the Roosevelt-Churchill conference, they had decided to pursue the North Africa strategy, named Operation Torch.

Back in Washington, Eisenhower was preparing a strategic report for the military. When Eisenhower handed his report to Marshall, he was shocked when Marshall said, "You may be the man to execute it. If that's the case, when can you leave?" By June 24, Eisenhower was in London, as joint force commander of Operation Torch.

Once in Britain, Eisenhower was disturbed by the lack of trained troops and equipment. He was also convinced that the show of force needed to be so overwhelming that the surprise attack would neutralize the opposition.

It was a challenge to integrate American and British troops under one banner. The British were battle-hardened; the Americans were new to the fight. But Eisenhower was determined to make sure the troops would work together. "I will clamp down on anyone who tries to start any trouble between the Americans and British under my command," Eisenhower said. "There will be neither praise nor blame for the British as British or the Americans as Americans. We will fight it shoulder to shoulder. Men will be praised or blamed for what they do, not for their nationality."

Churchill went to Moscow in August 1942 and

explained to Stalin that there would be no second front in Europe in 1942. In the nearly four-hour meeting, Churchill presented the reasoning behind the decision to delay a direct assault on the continent. Stalin berated Churchill, blaming the Allied losses on a spinelessness and an unwillingness to take risks. "You must not be so afraid of the Germans," he lectured Churchill. Churchill controlled his temper, reminding himself of how much Stalin's people had sacrificed during the war. Stalin continued to argue his point, until Churchill cut him off, telling him the decision was final.

When the conversation turned to the mission in North Africa, Stalin became more interested. "May God help this enterprise to succeed," the Soviet leader said.

Roosevelt was a war president now. Churchill wore his heart on his sleeve and Stalin remained remote, but Roosevelt projected a steady and stable style. He was at his desk in the Oval Office every morning and throughout the day. He thought of himself as his own secretary of state, and often made unilateral decisions over the heads of his advisers.

FDR knew he needed a primary adviser to coordinate the army, navy, and air force operations. In July, he appointed Fleet Admiral William Leahy as chief of staff to the commander in chief of the army and navy of the

United States. Unlike modern presidential chiefs of staff, Leahy's job was primarily related to the military. Leahy had worked for FDR when he was assistant secretary of the navy.

At the time, the White House was a glum place, with heavy blackout curtains draped on the windows and gas masks stashed under desks. A fallout shelter had been built in the basement.

Roosevelt sometimes felt claustrophobic. He loved being out on the presidential yacht, but security officials considered it too dangerous because of the risk of a U-boat attack. He was forced to look for a retreat on land. Sixty miles north of Washington in the Catoctin Mountains of Maryland were several recreation sites that had been part of a WPA project during the Depression. In April 1942, FDR had driven to the topmost area and said, "This is my Shangri-La!" The government cleared the site and renovated the cabins for a presidential retreat. The result was beautiful while still keeping the rustic feel of the country. Roosevelt christened it a navy installation, the USS *Shangri-La*. (The retreat was renamed Camp David during Eisenhower's presidency, and presidents use Camp David to this day.)

During this time, Eleanor was often absent. She had purchased an apartment on Washington Square in Greenwich Village, New York, and she regularly spent two days a week there, doing business in the city. She enjoyed the independence and privacy this arrangement gave her. At the same time, she had increasingly become FDR's most valuable ambassador to the nation, not just with her daily columns but also with her frequent travels to meet the citizenry in person. She had come into her own. And although she often found herself in disagreement with her husband—over Japanese internment, for example—she never publicly spoke out against her husband's views.

In September, mindful of the upcoming midterm elections, FDR asked Eleanor to accompany him on a two-week train journey to visit defense plants and military facilities across America. She reluctantly agreed. In Detroit, they saw how the car industry had been turned over to war operations. The trip took FDR all the way west to a Boeing plant in Seattle, which would produce nearly 100,000 planes for the war effort.

After months of preparation, Operation Torch was set for November 8. The plan was to invade three ports—Casablanca, Oran, and Algiers—at the same time. "We were gambling for high stakes," Eisenhower recalled.

After France surrendered to Germany, two governments had formed: the resistance government, the Free French, which was under the direction of Charles de

Gaulle, and the Vichy French, which collaborated with the Nazis and had a heavy presence in North Africa. As he prepared for Operation Torch, Eisenhower worried about resistance from the Vichy French. He didn't know what to expect from them.

At 1:00 a.m. on November 8, the Allies landed. Eisenhower was thrilled that the troops faced less resistance than expected, although the fighting was far from over.

Eisenhower cut a deal with Vichy admiral Jean-François Darlan that if he would call his troops down, the Allies would support his authority in North Africa. It worked: the French military stopped fighting, and some joined the Allies. Without Vichy resistance, this part of the mission was accomplished within days.

However, in the Tunisian campaign that followed, large numbers of German forces mounted a defense. As Eisenhower battled on in Tunisia, back in America there was outrage over the deal with Admiral Darlan. How could Eisenhower work with a man who collaborated with the Nazis? It was a public relations nightmare. Roosevelt was concerned until he received a cable from Eisenhower, carefully outlining the reasons he made the arrangement. Roosevelt cabled back that Eisenhower had his full support, based on the fact that Eisenhower was on the ground and knew best. The issue ended when the admiral was assassinated in late December.

Delighted with the progress of the North Africa campaign, Churchill still warned: "Now this is not the end. It is not even the beginning of the end. But it is, perhaps, the end of the beginning."

FDR and Churchill hoped for a meeting with Stalin in early 1943, but Stalin refused. He said he couldn't leave during the battle with the Nazis in Stalingrad, which would end with more than a million Soviet deaths. FDR and Churchill decided to meet anyway near Casablanca.

Roosevelt arrived on January 14. Churchill was already in Casablanca. Eisenhower joined them, expecting to be criticized for having made the arrangement with Darlan. Instead, FDR and Churchill encouraged Eisenhower, and he felt cheered by their support.

The path forward remained a matter of debate. Stalin still demanded a second front in Europe in 1943. Churchill didn't think an invasion of France could be ready until 1944. Roosevelt and Churchill wanted the Allies to press on to southern Europe via Sicily, holding off on a direct assault on Western Europe until they were stronger.

They had to work out the issue of French leadership. FDR and Churchill had invited two French leaders— French military hero General Henri Giraud and leader of the Free French government, Charles de Gaulle—to join the conference. Neither stood out: Giraud was considered weak, with questionable support from French troops, while de Gaulle seemed more concerned with personal power than the good of the country. Churchill didn't like de Gaulle and suspected him of having fascist leanings. But Churchill and Roosevelt hoped to come up with a power-sharing arrangement between the two less-than-eager participants.

At first de Gaulle refused to go to Casablanca. When the British threatened to stop funding his Free French movement, de Gaulle agree to participate.

Giraud attended the conference, but he wasn't eager to share power with de Gaulle, either. To everyone's relief, on the last day of the conference, the two men set aside their power struggle in order to defeat Hitler. Roosevelt quickly arranged a photo opportunity, with the four of them—Roosevelt, Churchill, de Gaulle, and Giraud—together in apparent unity.

The leaders held a press conference. Roosevelt described the Allies' military readiness in glowing terms. In his remarks, FDR made a statement that would become the keynote of the conference:

Peace can come to the world only by the total elimination of German and Japanese war power . . . Some of you Britishers know the old story: we had a General called U. S. Grant. His name was Ulysses Simpson Grant, but in my, and the Prime Minister's, early days he was called "Unconditional Surrender" Grant. The elimination of German, Japanese and Italian war power means the unconditional surrender by Germany, Italy, and Japan. That means a reasonable assurance of future world peace. It does not mean the destruction of the population of Germany, Italy, or Japan, but it does mean the destruction of the philosophies in those countries which are based on conquest and the subjugation of other people.

Churchill didn't agree with the concept of unconditional surrender. But he stood by FDR, believing that he would never be able to negotiate with Hitler. FDR later admitted that the idea of insisting on unconditional surrender had come at the last minute. "We had so much trouble getting those two French generals together," he said, "that I thought to myself that this was as difficult as arranging the meeting of Grant and Lee—and then suddenly the press conference was on."

The hastily added words and the idea of unconditional surrender inspired heated public debate. It had never before been American policy to destroy the political systems of our enemies. Many experts worried that the declaration of no negotiations for peace could lengthen the war.

FDR arrived home to news that the Russians had triumphed at Stalingrad. Apparently, one prediction of Churchill's seemed to have come true. Back in May, he'd reminded his citizenry that Hitler's apparent dominance in Russia was deceiving. "He forgot about winter," Churchill boomed in a radio broadcast. In the end, the cold, exhausted, dispirited German forces were defeated.

Stalin still wanted the Allies to open a second front. How much longer could Stalin hold off the Germans? And although the United States and Britain had scored significant victories in Italy and the Pacific, it was a critical moment in the war, where bad choices could turn into defeat. Most important, the Allies had yet to confront the Germans in Western Europe, the setting where the war would be won or lost. As the Allied nations looked toward 1943, there was a grave awareness of being at the brink of the war's final, most decisive movement. They couldn't afford to get it wrong.

PART THREE

THREE DAYS AT THE BRINK

10

THE ROAD TO TEHRAN

SOVIET MARSHAL JOSEPH STALIN was furious. Once again, his plea for the Allies to open a second front in Europe had been dismissed. He thought the Western Allies were cowards, afraid to make the bold choices that would shift the momentum of the war to their side.

The Allies had first promised a second front in 1942. Then they put it off to 1943. Now they were pushing it back to 1944. After the war, Soviet foreign minister Molotov admitted that the Russians knew that the Allies weren't ready. They thought that by demanding help and being turned down, they were in a better position to ask for other support, such as arms and aircraft.

Stalin considered himself the hero of the war who received little credit. In a message to his armed forces on February 22, 1943, he said, "In the absence of a second front, the Red Army is bearing the whole weight of the war."

The remark angered United States ambassador William Standley, who held a press conference and accused the Soviets of downplaying the aid they were receiving through Lend-Lease. Stalin basically ignored him, communicating directly with Roosevelt and Churchill.

FDR tried to arrange a personal meeting with Stalin. He had discussed a meeting of the Big Three—Roosevelt, Churchill, and Stalin—but FDR wanted to first meet Stalin alone. He didn't tell Churchill about it, but he had previously written to the prime minister: "I know you will not mind my being brutally frank when I tell you that I think I can personally handle Stalin better than either your Foreign Office or my State Department. Stalin hates the guts of all your top people. He thinks he likes me better and I hope he will continue to do so."

FDR sent a message to Stalin asking for a meeting without Churchill. They tentatively planned to gather in Fairbanks, Alaska, but no date was confirmed.

Roosevelt also scheduled a conference with Churchill in Washington to discuss Italy and plans for a second front.

After the Washington conference, Churchill joined FDR for a trip to Shangri-La. Their time at the retreat gave the leaders a rare chance to relax. Churchill treasured their closeness and thought of them as brothers in arms. He cherished every opportunity to be with Roosevelt in private settings like this one. Sharing confidences, Roosevelt talked about the 1944 election and the possibility of running for a fourth term. Churchill was concerned about the prospect of Roosevelt leaving his job—and the war. But Roosevelt had not yet decided to run for a fourth term.

When Stalin learned of the conference between Roosevelt and Churchill, he was annoyed. Once again, he cited Russia's disproportionate sacrifice. "One must not forget . . . the tremendous sacrifices of the Soviet armies in comparison with which the sacrifices of the Anglo-American forces constitute a small quantity," Stalin wrote.

They still didn't have a date for a meeting between FDR and Stalin. FDR didn't mention the possibility of the meeting when Churchill visited, but the prime minister found out. When Churchill called to complain about being left out, FDR lied and said it was Stalin's idea.

★ ★ ★

Although Stalin still wanted a second front in Western Europe, he knew that the Italian campaign was the next logical battleground for the United States and Britain. Sicily was located across from North Africa and along the vital shipping lanes of the Mediterranean. Once taken, American and British forces could move north into Italy. The mission was planned for July 1943.

General Dwight Eisenhower decided to try a misinformation campaign. Calling together reporters, he described the plan of attack in detail, giving them the wrong point of the attack. They vowed silence, but the details leaked out, as Eisenhower knew they would. The Germans learned about the Sicily campaign, but they were preparing for an assault on the opposite side of the island. Even with this diversion, American and British forces encountered heavy resistance. Within hours, some 150,000 Allied troops had gained a foothold, and within 38 days, Sicily was in the hands of the Allies.

Allied successes in Italy created a domino effect that threw the country into turmoil. Italian prime minister Benito Mussolini's regime was toppled and he was jailed, though he was later rescued by Adolf Hitler's army. On September 3, Eisenhower signed an armistice agreement between the new Italian government and the Allies. Although fighting in Italy would continue for the rest of the war as Hitler's army counterattacked, the Axis would no longer have Italy officially on its side. It was a huge victory, which seemed to confirm Churchill's strategy of tackling Italy before Western Europe.

After meeting FDR in Quebec, Churchill and his twenty-year-old daughter, Mary, spent a few days with Roosevelt at Hyde Park, where they were treated to an all-American picnic of hamburgers, hot dogs, and large slices of watermelon. In the manner of parents everywhere, Churchill warned his daughter not to swallow any seeds, as they would grow into full watermelons in her stomach.

In Russia, Ambassador William Standley felt shut out of diplomatic efforts. In early May, he had sent a letter of resignation to the president; months went by before he was replaced. Standley believed that Stalin was engaged in a competition, not a collaboration. He thought that the Soviets weren't in the war to prevent Nazis from dominating the world. Instead, he thought Stalin regarded World War II as another capitalist war, and that it could be used as a stepping-stone toward their ultimate goal of world Communist revolution.

By the end of summer, it was clear there would be no meeting between Roosevelt and Stalin. On August 8, Stalin sent a handwritten letter to FDR stating that he could not meet outside of Russia. "I do not have any objections to the presence of Mr. Churchill at this meeting, hoping you will not have any objections to this," he wrote.

FDR immediately began planning for a Big Three conference. It began with a discussion about location. FDR suggested North Africa. Stalin refused, arguing that was too far. Stalin countered with Tehran. Roosevelt responded that Tehran was too remote.

Other suggestions were made, but Stalin replied: "Unfortunately, not one of the places proposed instead of Tehran by you for the meeting is suitable for me."

Roosevelt again insisted Tehran was impossible, adding, "It would be regarded as a tragedy by future generations if you and I and Mr. Churchill failed today because of a few hundred miles . . . Please do not fail me in this crisis."

Stalin suggested the meeting be put off until spring—unless Roosevelt and Churchill agreed to go to Tehran. Roosevelt finally gave in, writing to Stalin, "I have decided to go to Tehran and this makes me especially happy . . . The whole world is watching for this meeting of the three of us." The meeting was scheduled to begin on November 28, 1943, in Tehran.

FDR traveled to the conference on the USS *Iowa*, one of the largest battleships in the American fleet. The massive ship was escorted by three destroyers. On the second day at sea, FDR was on deck to watch an anti-aircraft drill being conducted on one of the destroyers. During the drill, a torpedo was accidentally released, heading directly for the president's ship!

The commander of the destroyer contacted the *Iowa*: "Torpedo defense! This is not a drill!" The *Iowa* changed course, barely dodging disaster. Instead of taking cover, FDR ordered his assistant: "Take me over to the starboard rail. I want to watch the torpedo." It exploded a thousand yards away.

Without further incident, the *Iowa* completed its nine-day journey. They were met by a distinguished welcoming party, including Eisenhower and FDR's two sons, Elliott and Franklin Jr. On November 22, the president made the 1,800-mile flight to Cairo, where he would meet with Churchill before going on to Tehran.

At that time, the Soviet Union had not declared war on Japan, so Stalin did not want to have a representative at the Cairo meeting, where Roosevelt and Churchill would meet with Generalissimo Chiang Kai-shek, the chairman of the Republic of China, to discuss the progress of the war with Japan. The central issue remained defeating Hitler in Europe.

It was Thanksgiving in the United States, and Roosevelt had brought frozen turkeys from Washington so they could have a traditional turkey dinner. Toasting the prime minister at dinner that night, FDR spoke movingly of the Thanksgiving tradition, when close families are united. He spoke about the history and meaning of Thanksgiving, concluding, "And of course this leads me to the thought that I, personally, am delighted to be sharing this Thanksgiving dinner with Great Britain's Prime Minister."

Churchill stood to offer his own toast, but Roosevelt stopped him. He wasn't finished. "Large families are usually more closely united than small ones," he went on, "and so this year, with the people in the United Kingdom in our family, we are a large family, and more united than ever before. I propose a toast to this unity, and may it long continue!"

As they shared fellowship into the evening, they set their cares aside, at least for the moment. It was one last celebration of Western friendship before they joined Stalin for the most important meeting of the war.

"Did I ever think when he was little that Franklin might be president?" Sara Roosevelt wrote. "Never, oh never!" However, from the day of his birth, on January 30, 1882, Franklin was the only star in his mother Sara's galaxy. (Franklin D. Roosevelt Presidential Library)

The Roosevelts: (front row seated) Anna, FDR, Sara, Eleanor; (back row) James, Franklin Jr., Elliott, John. (Franklin D. Roosevelt Presidential Library)

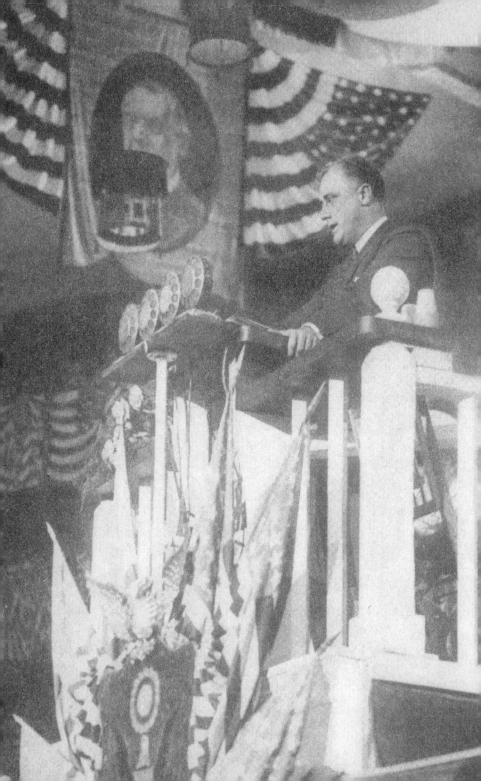

Left: Many believed FDR would never return to public life after he was struck with polio. But in 1924, he made a comeback. Gripping the podium to hold himself erect, he gave a fiery speech on behalf of Al Smith at the Democratic National Convention. He was back. (Franklin D. Roosevelt Presidential Library)

As president, FDR was determined to shake things up. He instituted twice weekly press conferences right in the Oval Office, with reporters crowding around his desk. (Franklin D. Roosevelt Presidential Library)

September 1939: Germany's Adolf Hitler looks on as his troops invade Poland, triggering the Second World War. Three years later, the Axis Powers would control almost all of continental Europe. (Bundesarchiv)

"A date which will live in infamy"—the Japanese attack on Pearl Harbor, December 7, 1941, nearly obliterated the Pacific fleet. Pictured, the USS *West Virginia* being bombed. (Toland Collection/U.S. Navy Photographs)

The first draft of Roosevelt's speech to the nation after Pearl Harbor. In its opening line, he changed "a date which will live in world history" to "a date which will live in infamy." (Franklin D. Roosevelt Presidential Library)

DRAFT No. 1   December 7, 1941.

PROPOSED MESSAGE TO THE CONGRESS

Yesterday, December 7, 1941, a date which will live in ~~world history~~ *infamy*

the United States of America was ~~simultaneously~~ *suddenly* and deliberately attacked

by naval and air forces of the Empire of Japan ~~without warning~~ .

The United States was at the moment at peace with that nation and was

at its ~~continuing the~~ conversation with its Government and its Emperor looking

toward the maintenance of peace in the Pacific. Indeed, one hour after

Japanese air squadrons had commenced bombing in ~~Hawaii and the Philippines~~ *Oahu*

the Japanese Ambassador to the United States and his colleague delivered

to the Secretary of State a formal reply to a ~~former~~ message, ~~from the~~ *recent American*

~~Secretary.~~ *While* This reply ~~contained a statement~~ *stated* *it seemed useless* that diplomatic negotiations

~~must be considered at an end, but~~ *it* contained no threat ~~and no~~ *or* hint of ~~an~~ *war or*

armed attack.

It will be recorded that the distance ~~of Manila, and especially~~ of

Hawaii, from Japan makes it obvious that the ~~y~~ attack ~~were~~ *was* deliberately

planned many days *or even weeks* ago. During the intervening time the Japanese Govern-

ment has deliberately sought to deceive the United States by false

statements and expressions of hope for continued peace.

On November 29, 1943, Joseph Stalin, FDR, and Winston Churchill posed for photos before beginning the hard work of the Tehran Conference. (Franklin D. Roosevelt Presidential Library)

In Tehran, FDR and Joseph Stalin hit it off, sometimes making jokes at Winston Churchill's expense in order to cement their relationship. But the underlying debate over which strategy would win the war was deadly serious, and Churchill was often at odds with his counterparts. (Franklin D. Roosevelt Presidential Library)

On the eve of D-Day, General Eisenhower visited the 101st Airborne
Division as it prepared to take flight. He shook each man's hand and they
assured him he had no cause for worry. But he was fully aware that, for
good or ill, the next day would bring a turning point in the war.
(Franklin D. Roosevelt Presidential Library)

On June 6, 1944, the Allies launched the invasion planned in Tehran.
Operation Overlord was the decisive battle of World War II. Even now,
some seventy-five years after D-Day, we are moved by the raw courage
of the men who stormed the beaches at Normandy. Many did not survive, but the course of the war was shifted toward victory.
(AP Photo/Peter Carroll)

On April 11, 1945, FDR was in Warm Springs to rest and recuperate after the long journey to Yalta. A portrait artist snapped this photograph, which was the last to be taken. The following day FDR suffered a stroke and died, not living to see victory over Germany, which came less than a month later. (Franklin D. Roosevelt Presidential Library)

FDR loved novelty items, and they crowded his desk in the Oval Office: a set of Scottish terrier and West Highland terrier figures mounted on magnets, an elephant figurine, a Missouri mule figurine constructed of nuts and pipe cleaners—plus a photo array of his four sons in military uniform, a desk lamp, pens and pencils, and other tools. (Photo by Karl Rabe)

11

YOUR HOUSE IS MY HOUSE

AS PRESIDENT FRANKLIN ROOSEVELT approached the Big Three conference in Tehran, he felt pressure to bring the group together. The relationship between Roosevelt and British prime minister Winston Churchill was as strong as any that had ever existed between leaders of great powers. Roosevelt admired Churchill's passion, courage, and moments of genius. He appreciated having a collaborator he could trust, and he never once doubted Churchill's devotion to their common cause. They also shared a commitment to freedom and common decency.

But as much as he loved Churchill, FDR needed Soviet marshal Joseph Stalin. He needed the Soviet leader to hold his own against the Germans in Russia. He needed him to join the fight against Japan, which he had not yet agreed to do. Most of all, he needed him as a partner in a postwar world that would assure a lasting peace. Roosevelt knew he had to handle Stalin carefully. Left to his own devices, Stalin might exploit victory against Hitler to pursue his own power. FDR thought if they kept Stalin close and gave him respect, they could avoid a postwar calamity. Roosevelt's goal at the meeting was to make Stalin a full and willing part of the team.

Iran had an alliance with the Allies, but there were German sympathizers in the city, which caused some concern for the conference. The original plan was for Roosevelt to stay at the American embassy, which was a mile away from the Soviet and British compounds. Since the meetings would be held there, Churchill and Stalin would have to drive through Tehran's treacherous streets on multiple occasions.

The Secret Service had heard reports that Nazi para-troopers had dropped into the area and posed a direct danger to the conference. Most of the agents had been captured, but they couldn't be sure they had them all. The plan was for German assassins to wear Red Army uniforms and pose as part of Stalin's security team.

Because of the security concerns, when FDR arrived in Tehran, the Americans accepted Stalin's invitation to relocate to the Soviet compound. Stalin was eager to host the president. FDR was given the largest house in the compound, with Stalin taking a smaller one. Stalin remained suspicious of his capitalist allies, and he could closely monitor their activities if they were kept under his roof.

The Americans assumed they were surrounded by Soviet agents. "Everywhere you went you would see a brute of a man in a lackey's white coat busily polishing immaculate glass or dusting dustless furniture," said Secret Service agent Mike Reilly. "As their arms swung to dust or polish, the clear, cold outline of a Luger automatic could be seen on every hip."

FDR didn't mind the move and thought it could give him a chance to get closer to Stalin. Had he instead stayed at Churchill's compound, it would have created the impression that the two were working against Stalin.

The day after his arrival, the president moved to the Soviet compound. FDR was driven in an undistinguished car along side streets, while a full motorcade with a Secret Service agent posing as the president traveled along the packed streets as the crowds cheered.

As soon as Roosevelt was settled, Stalin arrived at his door, dressed in a sharply pressed formal military uniform, with red epaulettes on his jacket and red stripes on his pants. He greeted Roosevelt with a wide smile.

The instant physical impression was startling because of Stalin's height and his striking characteristics. He was short and burly, with a face pockmarked from childhood smallpox (Stalin once recalled that in his early days, peasants called him "Pockmarked Joe"). He had broken teeth and a withered left arm that was shorter than his right, from an accident in his youth, and his steely eyes did justice to his adopted name. FDR grinned back. Roosevelt observed Stalin with interest and caution. FDR wanted to assess Stalin's true intentions and trustworthiness.

Stalin asked Roosevelt if he had ideas for the topics they should discuss. Roosevelt suggested they start with more general conversations and let the themes develop. This was Roosevelt's plan—to open things up and see where they went, although the British and American advisers preferred a more scripted approach. The two leaders touched on a number of topics in their forty-minute conversation, including the difficulty of supplying distant fronts in the Soviet Union, Roosevelt's meeting with the Chinese, and Stalin's resentment that the French gave in to Hitler. FDR tried to direct the conversation, taking Stalin into his confidence and explaining Churchill's trigger points.

"What'd you talk about?" Elliott asked his father when he arrived at the compound the following day. "Or was it state secrets?"

"Not a bit of it," Roosevelt said. "Mostly it was 'How did I like my quarters?' and 'Thank you very much for turning over the main house to me' and 'What is the news from the eastern front?'"

"Measuring each other, eh?"

Roosevelt didn't like that characterization. "I wouldn't say that . . . we were getting to know each other. We were finding out what kind of people we were."

"What kind of people is he?"

"Oh," the president replied, "he's got a kind of massive rumble, talks deliberately, seems very confident, very sure of himself, moves slowly—altogether quite impressive, I'd say."

At 4:30 p.m., the first official session came to order in a large meeting room with heavy tapestries on the walls. FDR was wheeled to the "head" of the large round table, with the flags of the three nations arranged in a centerpiece. The table was set for twelve delegates, four for each of the principals, though Stalin brought only two.

FDR called for the meeting to start and welcomed the Russians as "new members of the family circle." He urged everyone to speak freely and expressed his hope for a successful meeting. Churchill added that their meeting "was the greatest concentration of power the world had ever seen." Stalin added his greetings and spoke of the great opportunities ahead.

Roosevelt began with a brief account of the American perspective on the war. Acknowledging that the Pacific issues were of greater impact to the United States than the others, he felt it important that all of them knew the stakes, especially since one million men and most of America's naval power were in the Pacific. He described the strategy as a war of attrition—sinking Japanese ships faster than they could be replaced.

FDR then turned to the topic that was foremost on everyone's minds: Europe. The plan for a cross-Channel invasion of Western Europe had been under discussion for more than a year, but it was always discussed as something they would do in the future, when they were completely ready. Now the time had come to decide if they were ready or not to launch the attack, named Operation Overlord.

Stalin said that the Russians believed that the best result would be yielded by a blow at the enemy in northern or northwestern France . . . Germany's weakest spot.

Churchill, who had a bad cold, argued in favor of fighting in Italy first, then southern France. Stalin doodled drawings of wolves in red pencil while the prime minister spoke. When Churchill was finished, Stalin dismissed Churchill's concerns. If British and American forces were spread too thin, with large operations in both Western Europe and the Mediterranean, it might impede their success. They should focus on the European mission because the other operations would be diversions. Churchill said it was important to first take Rome, hopefully early in the year, noting that if Rome was not taken, his own political future would be in jeopardy, as he would lose the confidence of the House of Commons.

Roosevelt listened as Churchill and Stalin made their respective arguments. When FDR finally spoke, it was in support of Stalin. He also believed that Operation Overlord must be the focus.

Churchill left the meeting feeling depressed and sick with worry. He had not expected Roosevelt to take Stalin's side against him, after all they had been through together. Churchill later reflected: "There I sat with the great Russian bear on one side of me, with paws outstretched, and on the other side the great American buffalo, and between the two sat the poor little English donkey, who was the only one who knew the right way home."

Chatting after the meeting, FDR's aides were surprised by Stalin. Most had come to the conference thinking of Stalin as a "bandit leader," but they found him intelligent and well-spoken. He could be direct and considerate of the viewpoints of his colleagues, although he could be rude and blunt if someone argued a position that was against Soviet interests.

Roosevelt hosted a steak-and-baked-potato dinner the first night. During dinner, after the obligatory toasts, the difficult topics carried on as before. Stalin seemed determined to provoke Churchill, repeating what he had told FDR earlier about France after the war. He then expressed his belief that Germany should be so weakened that it could not recover its prior strength.

Stalin also raised a question about the policy of unconditional surrender. He questioned the specifics: What were the terms? Could the demand for unconditional surrender force the Germans to dig in even more? These were legitimate issues, but not ones that could be resolved at the conference in Tehran.

In the middle of their discussion, Roosevelt turned green and bent over in pain. His doctor was called, and he was wheeled out. Stalin worried that the president had been poisoned. Someone else at the table wondered if FDR had suffered a heart attack. Would the conference be canceled? To everyone's relief, the doctor let them know that the president was suffering from indigestion, nothing more.

As the dinner broke up, Churchill took Stalin aside to a sofa in the corner of the room. He wanted to talk about life after the war. "Let us first consider the worst that might happen," Stalin said. He proposed a situation in which Germany lost the war but was not destroyed; the country could reorganize itself and launch a new war. He had a point: this was essentially what happened after World War I, when the fever of nationalism elevated Hitler and led to visions of world domination. Stalin feared that the same thing could happen within fifteen to twenty years of Germany's defeat in the present war.

"Nothing is final," Churchill said. "The world rolls on. We have now learnt something. Our duty is to make the world safe for at least fifty years by German disarmament, by preventing rearmament, by supervision of German factories, by forbidding all aviation, and by territorial changes of a far-reaching character. It all comes back to the question whether Great Britain, the United States, and the U.S.S.R. can keep a close friendship and supervise Germany in their mutual interest."

"There were controls after the last war," Stalin said. They had failed.

"We were inexperienced then," Churchill said. "It will be different this time."

Accustomed to totalitarian practices, Stalin thought the victors should step heavily on Germany and prevent it from achieving economic success or military growth. On this point, Churchill agreed, although he wasn't sure how that could be achieved. Stalin reminded him that the controls exerted on Germany after World War I were inadequate.

Churchill had a different idea. He imagined the Big Three Allies working together to prevent Germany from becoming a power center. History shows that the Soviet Union took a very different path after the war.

Always one to say what was on his mind, Churchill then dared to bring up the question of Poland. He pointed out that the Nazi invasion of Poland had been the trigger for Britain's entry into the war, and he wanted to see the country thrive after the war as a strong and independent nation. Churchill worried that Stalin would try to carve into that independence, establishing new borders out of concern for his own country's security. Stalin sidestepped the question. It was late, and Poland would not be resolved at this meeting.

12

CLASH OF TITANS

ON MONDAY MORNING, BRITISH prime minister Winston Churchill tried to set up a private meeting with President Franklin Roosevelt. After the disastrous meeting the previous day, he wanted to be sure they were still on the same side. He sent a message to FDR requesting that they have lunch together.

Roosevelt refused.

He sent an aide to explain to Churchill that he didn't want to have a private meeting that might make Stalin feel left out. FDR was also concerned about the rooms being bugged, and he didn't want the Russians to pick up a private conversation between him and the prime minister. (It was later confirmed that the rooms *were* bugged. Stalin was stunned when he reviewed the transcripts: surely the president knew he was being bugged, yet he spoke so openly. "It's bizarre," Stalin said. "They say everything, in fullest detail!" In fact, this was not the case, as FDR had avoided talking to Churchill in his private quarters, and it's likely that he deliberately said what he wanted Stalin to hear.)

To make matters worse from Churchill's standpoint, FDR had a second private meeting with Stalin. He urged Stalin to join the war against Japan—one of FDR's primary goals for the meeting—and Stalin assured him he would, someday. Stalin believed no promises could be made until Hitler was defeated.

FDR then leaned toward Stalin as if to keep the conversation secret and said he wanted to discuss the future of the world after the war. He shared an idea for three governing bodies that would assure the peace. One would be an assembly of United Nations members. A second would be an executive committee, composed of the United States, Great Britain, the Soviet Union, China, and representatives of two European nations, one South American, one Middle Eastern, and one British dominion; this group would address nonmilitary issues.

Finally, there would be a third body, what FDR called the "Four Policemen"—the United States, Great Britain, the Soviet Union, and China. This group would deal with breaches in the peace anywhere in the world.

Stalin didn't like the idea of the Four Policemen. He said China had no place in such an important body, and he thought smaller nations would never support it. He suggested an alternative: dividing the authority between one Western (European) committee and one Far East committee; the Americans could be a part of the European committee. Roosevelt replied that Congress would never allow the United States to join a European organization.

A special event was planned for 3:30 in the afternoon, before the second conference. At the ceremony, Churchill presented the "Sword of Stalingrad" to Stalin, in the name of King George VI, to honor the victory at Stalingrad. Handing the sword to Stalin, Churchill read a prepared statement: "I have been commanded by His Majesty King George VI to present to you for transmission to the City of Stalingrad this sword of honor, the design of which His Majesty has chosen and approved. The sword of honor was made by English craftsmen whose ancestors have been employed in sword making for generations. The blade of the sword bears the inscription: 'To the steel-hearted citizens of Stalingrad, a gift from King George VI as a token of the homage of the British people.'"

Stalin took the sword and kissed the scabbard. He passed it to his aide, who grabbed it nervously and, not expecting its weight, dropped it. The aide picked up the sword and Stalin handed it to FDR for his inspection. Everyone agreed it was a very fine sword.

The sword ceremony didn't improve relations between Churchill and Stalin. At the start of the session, the military staff presented a report from their morning meeting, which basically resolved nothing. The Soviets wanted to launch the European offensive as soon as possible, but no later than May 1, 1944.

Stalin directly asked: "Who will command Overlord?" He didn't trust that the operation was really being planned until a commander was named. FDR might have been tempted to name General George C. Marshall and put the matter to rest, but he held back.

Without a leader, Stalin didn't take the mission seriously. "Who bears the moral and military responsibility for the preparation and execution of Operation Overlord?" he asked. "If that is unknown, then Operation Overlord is just so much talk."

FDR ignored the insult, and replied calmly, "We know the men who will take part in carrying out Operation Overlord, with the exception of the commander in chief." Roosevelt whispered to an aide that he couldn't say because he hadn't made up his mind yet.

Churchill began a discussion about a broader strategy, including territories in the Mediterranean. It seemed to some that Churchill was opposed to a cross-Channel assault, ever. Stalin again dismissed Churchill's concerns, demanding that the focus remain on Overlord. He emphasized the importance of avoiding distractions that would take away from the primary operation.

FDR suggested that they discuss the timing for Overlord. The date May 1, 1944, had been suggested, and he thought they should stick with that, at least within two weeks.

Churchill refused to agree to that date. Once again, he insisted they consider the Mediterranean operations before firmly committing to an Overlord date.

Overlord first, Stalin said, again. The rest are diversions.

Churchill disagreed.

Finally, Stalin gave Churchill a hard look across the table. "Do the prime minister and the British staff really believe in Overlord?" he asked.

Silence fell over the room. Churchill narrowed his eyes at Stalin, and bit down hard on his cigar. "Provided the conditions previously stated for Overlord are established when the time comes, it will be our stern duty to hurl across the Channel against the Germans every sinew of our strength," he replied.

FDR tried to break the tension, waving his glasses in the air and recommending that they break for the very fine dinner Stalin was hosting. He suggested that the military committee meet the following morning to work through the details.

Stalin found the notion absurd. "Why do that?" he asked. "We are the chiefs of government. We know what we want to do. Why turn the matter over to some sub-ordinates to advise us?" But despite Stalin's reluctance, the military chiefs were told to go ahead with the task.

The group took a break before dinner. Roosevelt looked tired. He spoke with Elliott in his room, explaining that Stalin had reached the point where he looked at the prime minister as if he couldn't believe his ears.

"Our chiefs of staff are convinced of one thing," FDR told his son. "The way to kill the most Germans, with the least loss of American soldiers, is to mount one great big invasion and then slam 'em with everything we've got. It makes sense to me. It makes sense to Uncle Joe. It makes sense to all our generals. It's the quickest way to win the war."

The problem was, Churchill disagreed. FDR thought Churchill was too concerned about the Russians being strong in the postwar era. In fact, Churchill had a point. None of the Westerners wanted to address Stalin's true ambitions. It was easier to see themselves as having a common cause and to leave it at that, as long as the true goal was winning the war more quickly.

At the lavish dinner hosted by Stalin, the toasts went on endlessly. Between toasts and courses, the conversation turned once again to the postwar world. Churchill said Britain planned to keep Hong Kong and Singapore under British control, and it would maintain the territories it had before the war. He asked Stalin whether he would make territorial demands. Stalin, not wanting to enter that particular conversational danger zone, replied, "There is no need to speak at the present time about any Soviet desires. When the time comes, we will speak."

Roosevelt often joined Stalin in taunting Churchill. Like squabbling siblings, Stalin knew how to provoke Churchill, and he took the bait every time. When Stalin accused Churchill of wanting to go easy on Germany after the war, he got a reliable explosion from Churchill. Churchill was particularly incensed when FDR went along with Stalin's teasing. At one point he had dreamed of the time after the war when he imagined the United States and Great Britain as the Big Two in the world. Now he was faced with another possibility—that the United States and the Soviet Union would be the Big Two.

13

LIKE A RAINBOW

PRESIDENT FRANKLIN ROOSEVELT, BRITISH prime minister Winston Churchill, and Soviet marshal Joseph Stalin had decided to extend the Tehran Conference if they needed more time to reach an agreement, but the course of the conference was ultimately determined by the weather. An approaching cold front threatened to trap the leaders in the city if they didn't wrap up their business. They had only one full day left for plenary meetings.

On the morning of November 30, the American

and British chiefs of staff worked out a statement on the priorities of the war, agreeing to advance in Italy to the Pisa–Rimini line and to mount the largest possible operation in the south of France on the day of Operation Overlord (later known as D-Day). The exact date was to be determined based on the moon, tide, and weather conditions.

Just like that, the debate that had consumed the first two days of the conference was resolved. When the report was presented to Roosevelt and Churchill, they agreed and planned to discuss the arrangement with Stalin at lunch.

Before lunch, Roosevelt received a visit from the shah of Iran. The palace had first demanded that FDR visit the shah, but Roosevelt insisted the shah come to him. Despite having a reputation as a playboy, the young Reza Shah was serious and respectful. The shah was concerned about Iran's independence after the war, including control of its oil. The Big Three signed a statement supporting the rebuilding of Iran after the war, but history shows that they did not honor it. Britain's control of the nation and its oil ended only after the revolution in 1979.

After meeting with the shah, the three leaders gathered over lunch. Roosevelt told Stalin about the report ironed out with the chiefs of staff, and Stalin was happy with the results. He again asked who the commander of Overlord would be. FDR promised an answer in three or four days.

At 4:30 the leaders gathered for the final session of the conference. Now that they had an agreement, the mood was much more relaxed.

They talked about how to prevent the Germans from finding out about such a massive operation. Stalin described how the Soviets had built decoy tanks, airplanes, and airfields to trick German intelligence into thinking operations were planned in places where they weren't. He said that they had used as many as five thousand fake tanks and two thousand fake airplanes to confuse the Germans. He also said the Red Army broadcast false information in radio communications to mislead the Germans.

"Truth deserves a bodyguard of lies," Churchill said.

Stalin nodded. "This is what we call military cunning," he said.

Churchill said it was military *diplomacy*, adding that the three powers should work together to use deception and propaganda.

The afternoon session was briefer than the others, meant to put their stamp on the agreement made by the chiefs that morning. They decided that before Roosevelt flew out the following evening, the three of them would meet to talk again.

The main event on the third day was Churchill's gala birthday dinner at the British embassy. Churchill hoped the dinner would be a highlight of the conference. Elegantly dressed Persian waiters swept through the room. The tables were so elaborately set that Stalin privately grumbled about not knowing which of the many forks to use.

Churchill toasted the Soviet leader as "Stalin the great." As Stalin offered a toast, the lights dimmed and a waiter came walking toward them, holding a giant tower of ice cream set in ice and lit from within with a candle. As the waiter passed Stalin, the tower tipped and the ice cream quickly melted from the heat of the candle. The dessert exploded onto the table, covering Stalin's translator with drippy ice cream. Despite the mishap, everyone remained in high spirits.

Churchill, eager to make a gesture toward Stalin, noted that their different views were all a matter of tints, and that England was looking "a trifle pinker" these days—meaning more supportive of the Communist state. Stalin smiled, delighted. "This is a sign of good health," he announced. Roosevelt picked up on the theme, describing the differences of those around the table as being like a rainbow, which in America was "a symbol of good fortune and hope."

"We have proven here at Tehran that the varying ideals of our nations can come together in a harmonious whole, moving unitedly for the common good of ourselves and the world," Roosevelt said. "So, as we leave this historic gathering, we can see in the sky, for the first time, that traditional symbol of hope, the rainbow."

FDR wasn't content. After three days in Tehran, he still didn't feel as if he'd broken through to Stalin. Stalin had been courteous and agreeable—and, most important, he had signed off on the joint plan—but it didn't feel like enough to FDR. He wanted to achieve a relationship that felt more like friendship. Roosevelt didn't want to leave Tehran without creating that connection.

Late in the day, when the Big Three met informally, Roosevelt said to Churchill as they entered the room, "Winston, I hope you won't be sore at me for what I am going to do."

From the moment he entered the room, FDR made jokes at Churchill's expense. He teased him about his Britishness, his cigars, and his habits. Churchill was ruffled and Stalin smiled. Roosevelt kept at it until Stalin laughed, and then he called him Uncle Joe. "He would have thought me fresh the day before," Roosevelt said. "But that day he laughed and came over and shook my hand."

For the sake of Overlord, for the sake of winning the war with Japan, Roosevelt was willing to link arms with Stalin—who represented a clear future threat to American democracy—and dismiss Churchill, believing he could sort out their relationships at a later time.

Churchill was insulted. But FDR didn't feel he had any choice. He and Churchill had arrived in Tehran having already held five conferences between them. Churchill had been a guest at the White House, at Hyde Park, and at Shangri-La. They had become the most famous couple in the world. If they had flaunted their friendship, Stalin would have felt left out. That could have been disastrous. FDR had come to Tehran with the goal of winning Stalin over, but it wasn't easy to break through his defenses. Provoking a laugh from Stalin was a moment of success for FDR. He thought a man who laughed with you from the heart could be a true ally.

FDR's behavior might have seemed a betrayal to Churchill, but he thought the prime minister could take it in light of the greater purpose. In the end, Roosevelt figured, they'd achieved what they set out to do with the course of the war.

When the conversation turned serious, the three leaders discussed the future of Poland. Earlier, FDR had privately told Stalin not to expect him to weigh in on this sensitive matter. There was a presidential election coming up in 1944, and although he didn't want to run again, the war might force him to do so. In that case, he had to consider the six to seven million Americans of Polish heritage whose votes would be jeopardized if he made any declarations about the country's future. In that conversation, FDR could have pushed for Poland's independence and set limits on future Soviet expansion, but he didn't say anything for political reasons.

Stalin said he considered Poland a Russian concern, since it involved Russian borders and security. He also had trouble with the Polish government-in-exile, which had been formed in 1939. Although technically aligned with the Allies, the government-in-exile had been a thorn in Stalin's side. After the Soviet invasion of Poland, thousands of captured Polish officers and soldiers had been executed and buried in mass graves. The government-in-exile was involved in bringing the mass graves to public attention, and the Nazis took advantage of the bad publicity to shame the Soviets. (History has shown that Stalin had signed off on the massacre.)

The conversation then returned to Germany. FDR proposed a plan he'd been thinking about for some time, dividing Germany into five parts after the war. These five parts would be self-governed and divided into two regions for the purpose of United Nations or international control.

Churchill preferred a simpler plan, with the southern

German regions combined into a confederation.

Stalin disagreed. Germans were Germans, no matter how many parts you divided them into, he said. Overall, he preferred FDR's plan, as long as Germany was fully and completely dismembered.

A last worry nagged at Churchill. Was Stalin asking for Europe to be made up of small, weak states?

Not at all, Stalin said. He wanted a weak Germany, not a weak Europe. But was that actually true? With small and compromised European countries, the Soviet Union would be the only important military and political force in Europe. Stalin was always careful to say the right thing about his desire for peace and his respect for the independence of others, but he wasn't particularly trustworthy. FDR and Churchill gave him leeway because they didn't want to rock the boat.

At a quick ceremony before leaving Tehran, FDR, Churchill, and Stalin signed the Declaration of the Three Powers. It read, in part:

> *The common understanding which we have here reached guarantees that victory will be ours . . . We have reached complete agreement as to the scope and timing of the operations to be undertaken from the east, west and south.*
>
> *We express our determination that our nations shall work together in war and in the peace that will follow.*

159

And as to peace—we are sure that our concord will win an enduring Peace. We recognize fully the supreme responsibility resting upon us and all the United Nations to make a peace which will command the goodwill of the overwhelming mass of the peoples of the world and banish the scourge and terror of war for many generations . . .

Our attack will be relentless and increasing.

Emerging from these cordial conferences we look with confidence to the day when all peoples of the world may live free lives, untouched by tyranny, and according to their varying desires and their own consciences.

We came here with hope and determination. We leave here, friends in fact, in spirit and in purpose.

ROOSEVELT, CHURCHILL and STALIN
Signed at Tehran, December 1, 1943

The declaration "sounds like generalities," Roosevelt later told his staff. "But there is meaning in every sentence." And, he added, he believed that Stalin meant every word of it.

"Well, Ike, you are going to command Overlord," Roosevelt said when he greeted General Dwight Eisenhower in a stopover in Tunis after the conference. Eisenhower, who had expected orders to return to Washington, was shocked. Churchill and Stalin had favored General

George C. Marshall. But as FDR had told Marshall in breaking the news, "I feel I could not sleep at night with you out of the country."

Eisenhower grasped the nature of the assignment. "Mr. President," he replied, "I realize that such an appointment involved difficult decisions. I hope you will not be disappointed."

FDR made the long journey home, arriving in Washington on December 17. He had been away almost a month. His cabinet and staff gathered to greet him at the south entrance of the White House. He emerged looking tired but elated. "I do not remember the president looking more satisfied and pleased than he did that morning," Rosenman reported. "I never saw that same expression again."

PART FOUR

THE ENDGAME

14

AT LAST, OVERLORD

PLANNING FOR OPERATION OVERLORD consumed the early months of 1944. Everyone knew what was at stake: D-Day was the best shot at winning the war. General Dwight Eisenhower wrote to the combined chiefs of staff, "Every obstacle must be overcome, every inconvenience suffered and every risk run to ensure that our blow is decisive. We cannot afford to fail."

At his headquarters in London, Eisenhower was so busy entertaining dignitaries, including Churchill, that he decided to move to the outskirts of the city to

Kingston, staying at the humble Telegraph Cottage. (An amateur artist, he would later paint a wistful portrait of Telegraph Cottage, where he had planned D-Day.)

"For the sort of attack before us we had no precedent in military history," he wrote. "Caesar and William the Conqueror had crossed the Channel to invade England successfully. But the England of that day was not guarded by an almost unbroken perimeter of guns and fighting men."

The invasion looked deceptively simple, at least on paper. The airborne divisions would launch after midnight, dropping thousands of paratroopers inland to take the nearby towns and secure a beachhead. At dawn, the infantry would move from transport ships to landing crafts about ten miles offshore, before heading in waves to five beaches—Utah and Omaha (led by the Americans), Sword and Gold (led by the British), and Juno (led by the Canadians). They would be supported by amphibious tanks and gunfire from naval destroyers, which would move into position as close as possible to the beaches. Constant air strikes would clear a path for the invaders to move into the countryside. The infantry would take the beaches and push inland.

For the mission, Eisenhower needed the best commanders he could find. He carefully considered who should be the commander of ground forces on D-Day and decided on British general Bernard Law Montgomery. Montgomery had a reputation for being arrogant and difficult. He also thought himself better than Eisenhower, once saying, "Nice chap. No soldier." But Eisenhower was able to set aside the personal to choose the best person for the job.

"General Montgomery has no superior in the most important characteristics," Eisenhower wrote. "He quickly develops among British enlisted men an intense devotion and admiration—the greatest personal asset a commander can possess. Montgomery's other outstanding characteristic is his tactical ability . . . he is careful, meticulous, and certain." Eisenhower made his decision based on the good of the mission.

The timing for the operation was critical. The date was dependent on the tides and the lunar calendar; the Allies wanted to invade in darkness to minimize the risk of being seen. The best dates were determined to be June 5 to 7; the team chose June 5.

Despite the heavy burdens of command, Eisenhower visited the troops when he could. He didn't view them as part of a war machine who would storm the beaches as a powerful whole, but as individuals of flesh and blood who were prepared to make the ultimate sacrifice. When he shook hands with his soldiers, they promised to win for him.

Eisenhower met regularly with Churchill, who worried about the invasion. "When I think of the beaches of Normandy choked with the flower of American and British youth, and when, in my mind's eye, I see the tides running red with their blood, I have my doubts . . . I have my doubts," he told Eisenhower.

Churchill expressed more hope as the date approached. "General," Churchill said to Eisenhower, "if by the coming winter you have established yourself with your thirty-six Allied divisions firmly on the Continent, and have the Cherbourg and Brittany peninsulas in your grasp, I will proclaim this operation to the world as one of the most successful of the war. And if, in addition to this, you have secured the port at Le Havre and freed beautiful Paris from the hands of the enemy, I will assert the victory to be the greatest of modern times."

Eisenhower replied: "Mr. Prime Minister, we expect to be on the borders of Germany by Christmas, pounding away at her defenses. When that occurs, if Hitler has the slightest judgment or wisdom left, he will surrender unconditionally to avoid complete destruction of Germany."

At a final conference in London on May 15, with King George VI in attendance, Eisenhower and his generals described the plan for the mission. Afterward, Churchill told Eisenhower he planned to watch the landings from a naval ship in the Channel. Eisenhower argued against it; he didn't want to have to worry about the prime minister's safety while running the mission. The king told Churchill he wanted to go, too, which finally put an end to the idea.

Days before the operation, an air commander urged Eisenhower to abandon two of the easternmost airborne operations for fear of "futile slaughter." He said the casualties from these divisions would be catastrophic, and many thousands of men would die in an effort that would not substantially affect the outcome of the operation.

"I went to my tent alone and sat down to think," Eisenhower recalled. "Over and over I reviewed each step . . . I realized, of course, that if I deliberately disregarded the advice of my technical expert on the subject, and his predictions should prove accurate, then I would carry to my grave the unbearable burden of a conscience justly accusing me of the stupid, blind sacrifice of thousands of the flower of our youth."

On the other hand, Eisenhower knew that if he canceled part of the mission, it would upset the whole. He ultimately had to trust his own judgment. The entire mission would go forward as planned.

The one thing they could not plan for was the weather. On June 4, the day before the launch, the forecast was for foul weather. The operation's chief meteorologist told Eisenhower that a storm was coming in across the Channel. He recommended Overlord be delayed to June 6, but he couldn't guarantee the weather would be clear on that day, either. If they missed both dates, the next opportunity was weeks away, because of the tides. Eisenhower had to decide whether to go on June 6 and risk the lives of the troops in stormy waters, or miss the chance altogether. It was the kind of command decision no leader ever wants to make, and he decided to sleep on it for a few hours.

Eisenhower got up at 3:30 a.m. on June 5, and the meteorologist said the weather outlook for June 6 had improved. "Okay, we'll go," Eisenhower said.

That evening he traveled fifty miles away to Newbury, the staging area for the 101st Airborne Division. Hundreds of paratroopers were preparing for the jump of their lives. He stayed there until the last man took flight.

He returned to the base to wait for news. Earlier that day he had written a note, which he folded into his wallet, accepting full responsibility if Operation Overlord failed. He wrote: "Our landings in the Cherbourg-Havre area have failed to gain a satisfactory foothold and I have withdrawn the troops. My decision to attack at this time and place was based upon the best information available. The troops, the air, and the navy did all that Bravery and devotion to duty could do. If any blame or fault attaches to the attempt it is mine alone."

Eisenhower was not aware that the Germans knew the Allies were going to attempt a landing somewhere in Europe, but they were convinced they would not risk a Channel crossing at that time. "There's not going to be an invasion," German general Erwin Rommel told his troops with confidence. "And if there is, they won't even get off the beaches."

In the dark of night, the airborne divisions took off by the hundreds. Their formations were so tight that they risked running into each other as they began to be hit by German antiaircraft fire. Some planes exploded in flames. One paratrooper later recalled that as he looked out the open door of his plane, preparing to jump, the plane to his left disintegrated in a ball of fire.

The formation broke, sending many of the planes off course, and some came in lower than recommended for a jump. Jumping from lower altitudes, some paratroopers broke their legs or sprained their ankles landing in flooded marshes behind the beaches. Some were tangled in trees, and one paratrooper was caught on a church steeple and hung there for two hours before being captured by the Germans. The vision of an overwhelming landing force was dashed as paratroopers were spread across Normandy. Throughout the night, in ones and twos and then in small groups, the soldiers found each other and began to beat back the German resistance, capturing the town of Sainte-Mère-Église, one of their prime objectives. They had suffered heavy losses parachuting in, but had mostly achieved their mission.

At dawn, the convoys began their surge toward the beaches. High winds and a choppy sea battered the seasick soldiers as they approached, wet and cold, the waves crashing around them. Many young men—just nineteen, twenty, or twenty-one years old—saw their first combat of the war in that desolate spot.

The divisions headed to Utah Beach, the westernmost location, were faced with currents so strong they were pushed off course by more than a mile. Teddy Roosevelt's son, Brigadier General Theodore Roosevelt Jr., at age fifty-six the oldest man on the beach, was among the first to reach land. Seeing they were off course, he called out, "We'll start the war from here!" In fact, the mistake proved fortunate, as there were few enemy forces at that end. By noon they were off the beach and four miles inland.

On Gold Beach, there was heavy initial fire, although aerial bombings had done their job of weakening resistance. An hour after landing, the British were headed inland. Canadian soldiers landing at Juno Beach were hit with a devastating assault by Germans firing from behind bunkers, but they were quickly able to get off the beach. British and Canadian soldiers landing at Sword Beach encountered little firepower, but faced a fierce battle in the countryside.

The Americans headed to Omaha Beach encountered a horrifying spectacle. The beaches were heavily reinforced with stakes, barbed wire, mines, steel barriers, and concrete walls. Worse still, a well-armed German division fired down from the bluff above the beach, easily stopping the first wave of infantrymen to reach the shore. Other Americans were swamped in the water, weighed down by up to ninety pounds of arms and equipment. Dunked in deep water, some men lost their rifles and ammunition, and others drowned in the powerful waters.

The expected bombing support from the air did not happen because the commanders were concerned about hitting the American troops. With the death toll mounting and the survivors trapped on the beach, the commander of the American ground forces briefly considered abandoning Omaha, which would almost certainly have meant the failure of Overlord. Only the supreme courage and strength of the infantrymen saved the situation. With many of their officers lying dead or wounded, they decided to press on toward the

German division, where they were able to overwhelm their opponents. By early afternoon, the Americans had taken Omaha Beach, but thousands of their brothers in arms lay dead on the beach and in the water.

Almost ten thousand soldiers died during the Overlord launch, and thousands more were wounded. Victory came at a heavy price.

In America and England, people listened to radio reports from the front. The coverage had started in the early hours of June 6, with the BBC announcing, "D-Day has come." At 3:40 a.m., Edward R. Murrow read Eisenhower's Order of the Day, which had been delivered to the Overlord forces: "The tide has turned. The free men of the world are marching toward victory." This was followed soon after by Eisenhower's own voice, speaking to the Europeans: "People of Western Europe . . . the hour of your liberation is approaching."

One of the most riveting reports came just before 6:00 a.m., when a live feed was linked to the networks by a reporter aboard an American ship three miles from the coast. With the sounds of bombs and firing in the background, he reported it all: "Very heavy firing now off our stern . . . fiery bursts . . . the whole seaside is covered with tracer fire . . ." until finally, the sounds died down. "Well, it's quiet for a moment now," the reporter said with remarkable calm. "If you'll excuse me, I'll just take a deep breath for a moment and stop speaking." He paused, until the firing started again.

President Franklin Roosevelt was awake in the small hours of the night, and he was relieved to receive Eisenhower's early report, with its premature but ultimately accurate conclusion that Overlord was a success. That night, rather than making a speech, Roosevelt delivered his message over the radio in the form of a prayer: "Almighty God: Our sons, pride of our nation, this day have set upon a mighty endeavor, a struggle to preserve our Republic, our religion, and our civilization, and to set free a suffering humanity. Lead them straight and true; give strength to their arms, stoutness to their hearts, steadfastness in their faith . . . Their road will be long and hard . . . They fight not for the lust of conquest. They fight to end conquest. They fight to liberate. They fight to let justice arise . . ."

In England, Prime Minister Winston Churchill addressed the House of Commons with two pieces of good news. The first was the liberation of Rome, which had occurred on June 4. The second was the early success of Overlord. That afternoon he cabled Soviet marshal Joseph Stalin: "Everything has started well. The mines, obstacles, and the land batteries have been largely overcome. The air landings were very successful, and on a large scale. Infantry landings are proceeding rapidly, and many tanks and self-propelled guns are already ashore." He later followed up with a fuller account describing the "serious difficulty" encountered at Omaha Beach.

Stalin telegraphed a few days later. "History will record this deed as an achievement of the highest order," he wrote.

Everyone knew there was a long fight ahead. "From the start of Overlord, we knew that we would win—but we knew it not factually but with faith," Eisenhower wrote. "When the Nazis' situation was hopeless, by any rational standard, they could still explode into fitful snatches of energy and deadliness. With the Russians on the east, and the Western Allies driving in from the other side, only in the frenzied mind of Hitler and those hypnotized by him could there have been the expectation of lightning strikes that would liberate Germany from our tightening, encircling armies."

After D-Day, Eisenhower never doubted that the Allies would win. But the Germans weren't giving up and the war was not yet over.

15

FDR'S FINAL ACT

PRESIDENT FRANKLIN ROOSEVELT WAS the only president in the history of the United States to serve a third term, and now he was considering running for a fourth. At age sixty-two, many people thought he looked at least ten years older, and some wondered if he could survive another four-year term. FDR suffered a bronchial infection after the conference in Tehran, but given his pale complexion and rapid weight loss, some feared he was more gravely ill.

"I found the Boss occasionally nodding over his mail

or dozing a moment during dictation," his secretary Grace Tully recalled. "At first I was surprised but I considered it merely a fatigue of the moment. He would grin in slight embarrassment as he caught himself and there was no diminution of clarity or sparkle in his words or in his thoughts. But as it began to occur with increasing frequency I became seriously alarmed. It was evident that the grind was becoming too severe for him . . ."

FDR's press secretary had to field questions about the president's health, but he had nothing to tell them. On March 27, 1944, FDR went quietly to Bethesda Naval Hospital. A navy cardiologist examined him and diagnosed several conditions, including gallstones, an enlarged heart, high blood pressure, and hypertensive heart disease. The doctor recommended a recovery program that would have had FDR laid up for months, but the president insisted on continuing with his regular routine. The report passed on to the nation was that he had a bad cold, which was the truth but not the *whole* truth.

FDR was also engaged in another deception: he had renewed his relationship with Lucy Mercer. After Eleanor had discovered their affair in 1918, Lucy had left town and become governess to a wealthy New York widower, Winthrop Rutherfurd, who had six children. Although Rutherfurd was almost thirty years her senior,

Lucy married him in 1920, and they had one child of their own. By all accounts, the marriage was a good one, but Lucy and the president kept up a correspondence. Lucy's first secret visit to the White House occurred in 1941 under the name Mrs. Johnson.

After Rutherfurd died in 1944, Lucy's relationship with the president grew closer. FDR's friends and his daughter Anna helped arrange secret meetings between the two. Anna agonized over keeping such an important secret from her mother, but she concluded that her father needed Lucy's companionship. The relationship between Eleanor and FDR was complex and often caused stress between the two. Eleanor cared passionately about the nation's problems, and when she saw her husband, she often confronted him with her concerns. But their personal relationship was distant.

Once again, FDR refused to announce his plans to run for another term until the party leaders were banging their heads against the walls in frustration. Most people expected him to run, in spite of his health, because of the war. "Mr. Roosevelt did not want to run for a fourth term," said wire service reporter Merriman Smith. "Age was beginning to tell on him. He had lost much of his vitality. The specter of illness was increasingly visible. But it was a thing he had to do. He was like a fire horse refusing to go to pasture."

When he finally announced that he was running—again—no one was surprised.

At their convention in Chicago, the Republicans nominated moderate New York governor Thomas Dewey, twenty years Roosevelt's junior. Although he was younger, he wasn't a particularly appealing candidate. "The man had one of the coldest personalities of anyone who had ever contemplated a run for the American presidency," wrote biographer David M. Jordan. Dewey was also running against a war president while the war was going well.

At the Democratic convention in July, the only question was who would be FDR's vice president. For his third term, FDR had replaced vice president John Nance Garner with Henry Wallace, his secretary of agriculture. FDR wanted to keep Wallace for his fourth term, but many Democrats thought he was too liberal for the party. This was an important decision because Roosevelt's fourth-term vice president might become president if FDR didn't complete the term.

Roosevelt considered other options. The chairman of the Democratic National Committee suggested two names: Supreme Court justice William O. Douglas and Missouri senator Harry S. Truman. Roosevelt agreed to accept either. In a note to the chairman, FDR put

Douglas's name first and Truman's second, but at the last minute he asked Grace Tully to retype the letter and switch the names—Truman first and Douglas second. He also said he had no problem with Wallace putting his name before the convention. In truth, FDR barely knew Truman, who later complained that the White House had not been very good about returning his calls when he was in the Senate.

Hearing that his name was in contention, Truman wanted nothing to do with it. "The Vice President simply presides over the senate and sits around hoping for a funeral," he told a friend. Even when people mentioned FDR's health and suggested that the vice presidency was a likely path to the highest office, Truman wasn't interested. He wrote to his daughter, Margaret, "1600 Pennsylvania is a nice address but I'd rather not move in through the back door—or any other door at sixty."

Despite the protests, Truman didn't object to being nominated at the convention. Seven more candidates were named, but it soon became clear that the real contest was between Wallace and Truman. After several ballots, Truman won the nomination with nearly unanimous support.

It was uncommon but not totally unprecedented for presidents to switch vice presidents. Both Thomas Jefferson and James Madison had done so, and FDR had already had two different vice presidents before he chose Truman. Soon after the convention, Truman was invited to the White House for lunch with the president. They discussed nothing of consequence. They never would. Truman later said he and FDR had had only two meetings and never discussed the war plans or the development of the atom bomb—the most devastating weapon of war ever devised.

The former New York State Democratic chairman thought the party was being unfaithful to its principles by allowing Roosevelt to run for a fourth term. "Anyone with a grain of common sense would surely realize from the appearance of the President that he is not a well man and there is not a chance in the world for him to carry on four years more and face the problems that a President will have before him; he just can't survive another presidential term," the chairman wrote.

If the party believed that FDR wouldn't survive another term and his vice president would become president during the next four years, Truman might not have been the best choice. He had very little foreign policy experience.

FDR's physical frailty was on display at a disastrous campaign speech. He decided to stand during the speech, wearing the leg braces he rarely used anymore. Propped behind a podium on the deck of a destroyer, he looked shrunken and uncomfortable. The radio pickup was awful, making the president sound as if he were mumbling and dropping syllables. Instead of hiding his weakness, it was on full display.

On Election Day, Roosevelt won, but not by a landslide. Although he received 432 electoral votes to Dewey's 99, the popular vote margin was only a little over three and a half million. That night, knowing it would be his last election, FDR greeted neighbors and supporters on his front porch.

The inauguration was a modest affair, held on the South Portico of the White House. The previous inauguration had taken place before the United States entered the war. Now FDR had neither the time nor the energy to devote himself to an elaborate event. "Dog catchers have taken office with more pomp and ceremony," an aide observed.

Some worried that the president didn't have the strength for the job. The previous day, when he met with the press, he told them, "The first twelve years were the hardest." At the cabinet meeting that day, Labor Secretary Frances Perkins said she thought "his face looked thin, his color was gray, and his eyes were dull. I think everyone in the room privately had a feeling that we must not tire him."

After standing outside in the bitter cold to take his

oath, FDR stopped in the Green Room with his son James. He was thoroughly chilled and confessed he was experiencing stabbing chest pains. He had a drink and rested for a few minutes, then joined the reception as if nothing were wrong.

Two days later, he left for a second secret meeting with Winston Churchill and Joseph Stalin.

By the fall, it had become clear that there were some cracks in the coalition. Roosevelt had met with Churchill in September, and Churchill planned to visit Stalin in Moscow alone. FDR's advisers worried that Churchill could not speak for the United States, and they hoped he wouldn't try. FDR wrote to Stalin: "I am firmly convinced that the three of us, and only the three of us, can find the solution to the still unresolved questions."

Stalin replied that Roosevelt's message puzzled him. He assumed Churchill's visit was to discuss agreements reached with Roosevelt when they met earlier. Stalin was subtly trying to drive a wedge between Roosevelt and Churchill.

In Moscow, Churchill shared with Stalin his own plan for the future of Eastern Europe, a plan that was *not* approved by FDR. Churchill basically divided Eastern Europe between Britain (and presumably the United States) and the Soviets: Romania (90 percent Soviet,

10 percent Britain), Bulgaria (75 percent Soviet, 25 percent Britain), Yugoslavia and Hungary (both divided equally), and Greece (90 percent Britain, 10 percent Soviet).

Secretary of state Edward Stettinius was concerned about the Soviets and British tinkering with Eastern Europe. "We specifically desired a pledge by the Soviet Union and Great Britain that in liberated Europe free elections would be held and governments representative of the people would be established," Stettinius wrote.

Roosevelt proposed a meeting somewhere in the Crimea, a site under Soviet control. Stalin agreed.

By early 1945, the war on the eastern front was all but over, and the Soviet forces were moving west to join the Allies in Europe. Operation Overlord had succeeded beyond all expectations, putting Germans on the defensive. France was liberated in August 1944.

The Japanese had suffered a series of crushing defeats in late 1944. FDR hoped that the Soviets would soon join the Pacific War, hastening its end.

The Allied Powers were convinced the war was effectively won, so this conference would focus on building the peace. On January 22, FDR boarded the USS *Quincy* for the long journey. Churchill had convinced FDR to stop in Malta first for a short meeting on military strategy, and FDR agreed.

They were in high spirits but poor health when they met. Churchill had a fever, and FDR looked so thin and ill that everyone who saw him was alarmed.

Yalta had once been a glamorous place, a favorite vacation spot of Tsar Nicholas, but it was now nearly in ruins. Churchill thought it was a grim location for the conference. "If we had spent ten years on research, we could not have found a worse place in the world than Yalta," the prime minister told FDR. "It is good only for typhus and deadly lice who thrive in those parts."

It was also very inconvenient. Since the nearest airfield was ninety miles away, the original plan had been to bring Roosevelt to Yalta by ship across the Black Sea.

"You can't," the Soviet police told FDR's security team.

"Why?"

"Mines," the police replied.

"How many?"

"Who knows," the Soviet agent said. "The Germans put them there. They didn't leave a map."

FDR drove almost a hundred miles from the airport to Yalta, taking note of the destruction along the way. He later described it to Congress: "I saw the kind of reckless, senseless fury, the terrible destruction that comes out of German militarism. Yalta, on the Black Sea, had no military significance of any kind. It had no defenses. Before the last war, it had been a resort for people like the Czars and princes . . . Nazi officers took these former palaces and villas . . . and when the Red Army forced the Nazis out of the Crimea—almost just a year ago—all of these villas were looted by the Nazis, and then nearly all of them were destroyed by bombs . . ."

The conference meetings were held at the Livadia Palace, which had been restored. Stalin arrived a day later. Dinner the first evening was hosted by FDR and included a hearty spread of American and Russian foods. During dinner, the three world leaders quarreled about who should oversee the peace process. Roosevelt and Stalin thought the "peace should be written by the big powers." Churchill thought the smaller nations should have a say. He would continue to argue on behalf of smaller nations, despite his status as head of a colonialist power.

From the beginning, each of the Big Three wanted to make agreements that suited their own postwar needs. For Churchill, that meant maintaining the British Empire and preventing a strong nation from taking hold in Europe. For Stalin, it meant strengthening Soviet control in the East and having a presence in Europe that would assure Germany's inability to rebuild itself. For Roosevelt, it meant convincing Stalin to join the war against Japan and solidifying plans for an international organization that would protect the peace in the future.

Once again, Stalin strongly favored the complete dismemberment of Germany. He also argued that a high percentage of its resources should go to restore the nations it had destroyed, especially Russia. Neither Britain nor the United States favored reparations.

"If I could see any benefit in reparations I would be glad to have them but I am very doubtful," Churchill said. "Other countries also have suffered great devastation—France, Belgium, Norway. We must also consider the phantom of a starving Germany and who is going to pay for that. If our treatment of Germany's internal economy is such as to leave eighty million people virtually starving, are we to sit still and say, 'it serves you right,' or will we be required to keep them alive?" Churchill asked. "If you have a horse and you want him to pull the wagon you have to provide him with a certain amount of corn—or at least hay."

"But the horse must not kick you," Stalin's adviser replied.

Roosevelt tried to soothe Churchill, saying the American people did not want the Germans to starve, but they didn't want them to have a high standard of living, either.

In discussions about France, Churchill once again argued that France should be part of the postwar control machinery. Stalin disagreed. "I agree that the French should be great and strong but we cannot forget that in this war France opened the gates to the enemy. This is a fact. We would not have had so many losses and destruction in this war if the French had not opened the gates to the enemy. The control and administration of Germany must be only for those powers standing firmly against her from the beginning, and so far, France does not belong to this group."

Churchill defended France. "We were all in difficulties early in this war . . . I admit they were not much help in this war. But the fact remains they are the neighbor of the Germans and the most important neighbor. British public opinion would not understand if decisions vital to France are being made with regard to Germany over France's head. I hope, therefore, that we shall not decide for an indefinite exclusion of France for all time." Roosevelt sided with Churchill, and Stalin agreed to put France on the control council.

Much of the conference was spent discussing Poland. The temporary government in Lublin was very pro-Soviet. Stalin said the government was embraced by most of Poland, but that wasn't the case.

Churchill continued the argument that he had started at the Tehran Conference. "Britain declared war on Germany in order that Poland should be free and sovereign," the prime minister said. "Everyone knows what a terrible risk we took and how nearly it cost us our life in the world, not only as an empire but as a nation. Our interest in Poland is one of honor. Having drawn the sword on behalf of Poland against Hitler's brutal attack, we could never be content with any solution that did not leave Poland a free and independent sovereign state."

Stalin countered, "For the Russian people, the question of Poland is not only a question of honor but also a question of security . . . of life and death for the Soviet state."

Perhaps, Churchill suggested, the Big Three should create the terms for a new Polish government. Stalin disagreed. "I am called a dictator and not a democrat, but I have enough democratic feeling to refuse to create a Polish government without the Poles being consulted."

Roosevelt urged the organization of a provisional government, which would hold free elections as soon as possible. "How long before elections could be held?" Roosevelt asked.

"In one month unless there is a catastrophe on the front and the Germans defeat us," Stalin said. "I do not think this will happen."

Whether that timeline was realistic and whether the elections would really be free was a concern for Roosevelt. The Soviets now controlled Poland, and they probably would have been quite happy to keep it that way. But the American position was very strong that Poles should have self-determination. For his part, Churchill was suspicious about Stalin's declarations because the Western Allies didn't really know what was going on inside Poland and couldn't judge Stalin's claims for themselves.

The question of votes in the General Assembly—the proposed postwar governing body—was also difficult to resolve. Britain had six votes, representing its territories, and in that spirit, the Soviet Union ended up with three. This put the United States at a disadvantage, though Stalin offered to give the US two extra seats, an unsupportable idea. Roosevelt knew that Congress would be in an uproar over the extra seats for the Soviets.

In a private meeting, Roosevelt spoke to Stalin about Japan. Stalin had always said he would join the war against Japan once the Allies had achieved victory in Europe. Now Stalin was hedging. He told FDR that his people would not understand why the Soviets would go to war with a nation with whom they had no direct conflict. FDR dangled the opportunity for the Soviets to gain territory from Japanese conquests. "I only want to have returned to Russia what the Japanese have taken from my country," Stalin said, although he actually wanted much more.

Afterward, when the Soviets entered the war with Japan, they took control of several islands they had no right to. In the end, the Soviets reaped the benefits of victory over Japan, although it could be argued that they weren't needed to win the war, given the atom bomb.

Stalin and Churchill each envisioned a world shaped largely in their own prewar image: Great Britain with its empire and the Soviet Union with its tight control of a constellation of nations. Roosevelt had a different vision—a world beyond colonial "ownership," where independent states would be allowed to thrive, encouraged by a peacekeeping organization that would assure harmony in the world.

Privately, FDR resented Churchill's desire to protect colonial rule. American boys were not dying for the sake of the British Empire! Nor were they dying so the Soviet Union could retain its grip on the East. They were dying for freedom, for the dismantlement of imperial rule, for the emergence of opportunity and prosperity in every corner of the world.

The Big Three agreed that the first meeting of the United Nations should be held on April 25, 1945, in San Francisco.

At a dinner hosted by Stalin, everyone was in a good mood, and the toasts were more elaborate and flattering than ever. At some point, the flowery words began to sound hollow. "History has recorded many meetings of statesmen following a war," Stalin said in one toast. "When the guns fall silent, the war seems to have made these leaders wise, and they tell each other they want to live in peace. But then, after a little while, despite all their mutual assurances, another war breaks out. Why is this? It is because some of them change their attitudes after they have achieved peace. We must try to see that doesn't happen to us in the future."

Roosevelt added that he thought of the three nations as a family.

Churchill hosted dinner on the final night of the conference. The mood among the Americans was triumphant. But the British did not share the happy feelings. "It is the story of Teheran [*sic*] all over again," one of Churchill's aides wrote. "Stalin fights for and gets what he wants . . . Only a solid understanding between the democracies could have kept Stalin's appetite under control."

16

THE WORLD HE LEFT BEHIND

ON MARCH 1, 1945, President Franklin Roosevelt reported to Congress about the Yalta Conference. He spoke glowingly of the continued collaboration of the three nations. "Of course, we know that it was Hitler's hope—and the German war lords'—that we would not agree, that some slight crack might appear in the solid wall of Allied unity, a crack that would give him and his fellow gangsters one last hope of escaping their just doom. That is the objective for which his propaganda machine has been working for many months. But Hitler has failed."

Congress cheered. Americans could feel victory in Europe in their grasp, and the war with Japan seemed to be approaching the end as well. Now Roosevelt was consumed with the next stage, the time after the war. He planned to attend the first United Nations conference in San Francisco in April and to visit British prime minister Winston Churchill in London in May.

But he was worn out, and traveled to Warm Springs for a rest. He was accompanied by a small group—an aide, his secretary, his physician, and his cousin and confidante Daisy Suckley. Lucy Mercer Rutherfurd joined him later. Eleanor remained in Washington.

FDR did not find peace at Warm Springs. Despite his words to Congress, tensions were growing between the Big Three. State Department officials speculated that Soviet marshal Joseph Stalin had received heavy blowback from the Soviet governing authority, the politburo, for agreements made at the conference, and he was becoming less cooperative. In Warm Springs, FDR received an angry message from Stalin claiming that Russian intelligence picked up signs that the United States was trying to make a separate peace with Germany.

FDR responded that it simply wasn't true. "I feel that your information to that effect must have come from German sources which have made persistent efforts to create dissension between us to escape in some measure responsibility for their war crimes," the president wrote.

Stalin accepted the president at his word, more or less. "I have never doubted your integrity or trustworthiness," he wrote, although he had, and he did.

FDR also had reason to doubt Stalin's word. In the days after Yalta, the Soviets disbanded the Polish underground and set the stage for rigged elections. Roosevelt could only hope these matters would be settled in San Francisco.

Lucy arrived on April 9, and her presence eased FDR's mind. Still weak, he seemed to be slowly improving every day, and was even planning to attend a barbecue sponsored by the press on April 12.

Thursday, April 12, was a warm, sunny day. FDR woke with a headache and a stiff neck, which he eased with a hot water bottle. Lucy had commissioned an artist friend to paint a personal portrait of the president, and he was sitting for it that day. He emerged in a double-breasted gray suit and crimson tie, with a cape arranged over his thin shoulders to give him the appearance of heft. He was smiling and seemed happy. He looked well.

At 1:00, Roosevelt told the artist they had only fifteen minutes remaining. A few minutes later, the president swiped at his forehead and bent over. "I have a terrific pain in the back of my head," he said. Then he slumped forward, unconscious.

The president never regained consciousness. A heart specialist was called in from Atlanta, but as he was arriving, FDR's breathing grew heavy and then stopped. At 3:35 p.m., President Franklin D. Roosevelt was pronounced dead. The cause was a cerebral hemorrhage.

Lucy immediately packed her bags and left so she would not be there when Eleanor arrived.

Eleanor was at a benefit in Washington when she was called urgently to the White House. She was told her husband had died, then she stood stoically at Truman's side while he took the oath of office. She sent a message to her sons before leaving for Warm Springs: "DARLINGS: PA SLEPT AWAY THIS AFTERNOON. HE DID HIS JOB TO THE END AS HE WOULD WANT YOU TO DO. BLESS YOU. ALL OUR LOVE. MOTHER."

When she arrived at Warm Springs, Eleanor was crushed to learn that Lucy had been with her husband in his final moments. The renewal of their relationship had been kept secret from Eleanor for years, and she felt betrayed, most of all by her daughter Anna, who knew about the affair. When she saw Anna, she questioned her closely about Lucy. She blamed her daughter for being a part of the deception. It would take time for their relationship to heal. Eleanor's grief about her husband's death was complicated by the news of his infidelity.

FDR had not liked the practice of dignitaries lying

in state with crowds walking by to look at their caskets. His coffin was placed in the East Room of the White House, where the gathering was invitation-only. Off to one side sat his empty wheelchair. At one point, Eleanor requested a private moment, with the casket opened just for her. At another point, Harry Truman, now president, entered the East Room. Nobody stood. After a simple Episcopal funeral service, the coffin was placed on a train for Hyde Park.

In his funeral plans, Roosevelt had stated his desire to be buried in the rose garden at Hyde Park. Preparations were made for a burial on Sunday, April 15. A battalion from the Corps of Cadets at West Point was brought to Hyde Park, along with battalions from the army, navy, marines, and coast guard. The air force would fly in a formation above Hyde Park before the service.

Shoulder to shoulder, more than one thousand soldiers, sailors, and marines lined the route from the train station, saluting the flag-draped coffin as it passed on a caisson pulled by six horses. A riderless horse, draped in black, followed behind. Bugles played "Hail to the Chief." As the processional approached the gravesite, a twenty-one-gun salute boomed out, followed by the mournful chords of Chopin's funeral dirge.

Nearly two hundred close friends and relatives, along with assorted dignitaries, including President and Mrs.

Truman and their daughter, Margaret, crowded into the area around the gravesite. Several ministers were on hand, each reading a prayer. As the first prayer began, a single air force bomber that had circled back from the formation appeared overhead, dipping its wings in a salute.

Drums rolled as the casket was lowered into the ground, and cadets fired three volleys over the grave. The sorrowful notes of "Taps" were played as the commander in chief was sent to his final rest in the fragrant garden of the home he loved. A simple white stone marks the grave, inscribed with Roosevelt's name and dates and Eleanor's name and dates.

In Europe, General Dwight Eisenhower was directing the end of the war. His focus was on Berlin, Germany. Churchill wanted British troops to take Berlin, but Eisenhower thought that it was more practical for the Russian army to be the first to enter the city. He calculated that the approach could save fifty thousand lives. His goal was to win the war and minimize casualties.

As the Russians advanced on Berlin, they met little resistance from the Nazis, who were fleeing or surrendering to save their own lives. Hitler was hiding in an underground bunker with his longtime mistress Eva Braun and their two dogs. When he realized that defeat was inevitable, Hitler poisoned Braun and the dogs with cyanide and then swallowed a cyanide capsule and shot himself in the head. He left behind a last will and testament that read: "I myself and my wife—in order to escape the disgrace of deposition and capitulation—choose death."

On May 7—within a week of Hitler's death—Germany unconditionally surrendered. Germany's unconditional surrender with Russia was signed on May 9.

Eisenhower remembered how weary everyone felt after the surrender documents were signed. "When the signing finally took place, a little before three in the morning of May 7, I think no person in the entire headquarters gave much thought to starting a public celebration or participating in a private one," he wrote. "My group went to bed to sleep the clock around."

The Japanese were still fighting, refusing to accept that defeat was unavoidable. At a Big Three meeting in Potsdam, Germany, from July 17 to August 2, President Harry Truman, Churchill, and Stalin signed a declaration calling for the unconditional surrender of Japan. Privately, Truman informed Stalin that the United States possessed "a new weapon of unusual destructive force," which could be used against the Japanese if they refused to surrender. Stalin was pleased. Churchill already knew of FDR's atomic bomb program and agreed that it might be necessary. Truman was relieved at their response. He had only learned of the atomic bomb program after FDR's death—a big secret to keep from the vice president—but he said he would not hesitate to use it if it would end the war.

Eisenhower was at Potsdam when he learned about the bomb, and he felt sick. He urged Truman to offer the Japanese a way to end the war without using the bomb. But Truman stood firm, and unfortunately the Japanese refused to budge. On August 6, the United States dropped the first atomic bomb on Hiroshima, followed by a second bomb August 9 on Nagasaki. The horror exceeded the worst nightmares. Tens of thousands were instantly burned or crushed in their homes, with many thousands more dying slowly of burns and radiation sickness. With the city centers in ruins, homeless victims huddled in the streets, suffering, sick, and shocked by the destruction.

On September 2, Japan surrendered unconditionally. In an address to a stunned nation conditioned to *never* surrender, Emperor Hirohito explained that it was the only choice. "The enemy has begun to employ a new and most cruel bomb, the power of which to do damage is, indeed, incalculable, taking the toll of many innocent lives," he said. "Should we continue to fight, it would not only result in an ultimate collapse and obliteration of the Japanese nation, but also it would lead to the total extinction of human civilization."

A new form of warfare had been born, rising in the mushroom clouds over Japan's cities, replacing the bloody battlefields of World War II with a more frightening weapon that would dominate foreign policy for generations to come.

FDR had anticipated having years to build the peace. He had dreamed of a postwar era when he could be a moderating influence on Stalin. He expected the war-torn nations to be focused on rebuilding and weary of fighting, making them more willing to compromise.

FDR expected that he would be there to see it all through. With the San Francisco conference only weeks away, he was focused on how to heal the rifts that were developing after Yalta. Perhaps FDR expected the bomb to change the balance of power, unaware that the Soviet Union was well on its way to developing its own nuclear technology.

In Tehran, FDR brought Stalin into alignment with the West to win the war. He artfully negotiated with both Churchill and Stalin to support Operation Overlord, which paved the way for the war's end. It might be said that Tehran won the war, but Yalta failed to secure the peace.

Many have speculated since that Roosevelt was too ill at Yalta to do justice to the details of the negotiations. More likely, Roosevelt walked a fine line with Stalin, figuring he could bring Stalin around in future meetings. Roosevelt made the decision that the details could be ironed out later, and it was more important to present a united front while Germany and Japan were still on the offensive. When questioned at a press conference after Tehran about the details of the agreement, Roosevelt said, "We are still in the generality stage, not in the detail stage, because we are talking about principles."

When Secretary of State Edward Stettinius first met with Truman, he told him about FDR's difficult dealings with Stalin after Yalta, and his opinion that relations had deteriorated since the conference. Truman said that the United States must stand up to Russia. Truman's subsequent hostility when he met Stalin at the Potsdam Conference in July 1945 had a chilling effect on Soviet cooperation. "Roosevelt knew how to conceal his attitude toward us, but Truman—he didn't know how to do that at all," Molotov said in 1975. "He had an openly hostile attitude."

At this point, the Soviets stopped pretending to support certain freedoms discussed at the previous conferences.

Discussing the issue of free elections in Eastern Europe, Stalin said what he had believed all along. "A freely elected government in any of these countries would be anti-Soviet, and that we cannot allow."

Did FDR's concessions to Stalin at Tehran and Yalta set the stage for the Cold War?

If Roosevelt had lived, would relations with the Soviet Union have been better?

Did Roosevelt know that the Soviets were developing nuclear technology?

It's easy to forget in the aftermath of a long Cold War that the Soviets played a critical role in fighting Hitler. It's easy to forget how desperate the Allies were for victory—and that victory was not always certain. During World War II, Roosevelt needed Stalin.

Stalin presented a positive image of himself in Tehran and Yalta. The reasonable, friendly "Uncle Joe" of those conferences was a different person in Russia. Roosevelt and Churchill didn't know what was going on inside the Soviet Union, and they ignored signs that Stalin was hungry for Soviet expansion. In Tehran and Yalta, Stalin preached moralistically about the need to destroy Germany in order to prevent another Hitler, but in the process, he laid the groundwork for carving off the eastern part as a subject of the Soviet Union. His true aim was offensive, not defensive. He wanted control, and weak nations were easier to conquer.

In hindsight, some wonder why the American and British leaders ever believed that Stalin would allow fair elections and a free press in liberated Europe, when those same freedoms were denied to the Soviet people themselves. Roosevelt had convinced himself he could handle Stalin after the war. He ignored Stalin's contempt for democracy. FDR also believed that the Soviet Union would be so weak after the war that it wouldn't have the will to become an aggressor.

When the war ended, the change was immediate. At the moment of victory, Stalin returned to his old ways. Roosevelt was dead; Churchill was out of office. Stalin had little respect for Truman, and the Soviet Union was developing its own atomic bomb. Stalin spoke out against Western values and institutions, blaming capitalism for inspiring the rise of Hitler. When Roosevelt had spoken of self-determination, free elections, and a peaceful world, Stalin had nodded along and said he wanted that, too. Roosevelt's mistake was believing him. Stalin intended to do exactly as he pleased, regardless of anything he had promised.

After World War II ended, there was a great feeling of joy and optimism in the Western world. In the United States, the end of the war began a period of great prosperity and opportunity. Soldiers returning from battle were provided with benefits from the GI Bill, enabling them to go to college and purchase homes. In the eyes of many people around the world, FDR was to thank for restoring hope to a world that had been at the brink of disaster. He became a hero, and American polls still show him to be one of our greatest presidents.

But there were some consequences of the war that weren't positive. Once the United States dropped the atom bomb on Japanese cities, there was no stopping other nations from developing nuclear technology, including the Soviet Union. After Stalin became an open adversary of Western nations, the East and West entered into a Cold War, where the threat of a nuclear attack was ever present. Today, the possibility of a hostile nation developing nuclear weapons and using them is still a real threat.

It takes courage for nations to deal with these challenges. In 1982, President Ronald Reagan gave a speech before the House of Commons in London, reminding people of that: "During the dark days of the Second World War, when this island was incandescent with courage, Winston Churchill exclaimed about Britain's adversaries, 'What kind of people do they think we are?' Well, Britain's adversaries found out what extraordinary people the British are. But all the democracies paid a terrible price for allowing the dictators to underestimate us. We dare not make that mistake again. So, let us ask ourselves, 'What kind of people do we think we are?' And let us answer, 'Free people, worthy of freedom and determined not only to remain so but to help others gain their freedom as well.'"

— ACKNOWLEDGMENTS —

Like *Three Days in January* and *Three Days in Moscow*, *Three Days at the Brink* could never have been realized without the hard work, imagination, and dedication of my coauthor, Catherine Whitney. Catherine has the uncanny ability to throw herself into a project and absorb all of the details. Catherine scoured thousands of pages of library documents, oral histories, biographies, and notes from the Tehran Conference, and in the same back-and-forth process we used in the other two books, the result was a very readable and dramatic telling of an important three days in history and a look back at the life of one of our most consequential presidents.

Our industrious researcher, Sydney Soderberg, spent a lot of time at the Franklin Delano Roosevelt Library and Museum in Hyde Park, New York. The gems that Sydney was able to dig up provided the "crackle" in the detail and storytelling of that conference. A real-life drama told with the help of oral histories and notes from Tehran.

The professionals at presidential libraries provide a crucial role of preserving and protecting presidential history. And the treasures they hold inside can paint a picture of a moment or a presidency. The FDR Library and Museum opened its doors wide to me and the team. I would like to personally thank Paul Sparrow, the director of the library. Paul was enthusiastic about the project from the start and helped get everything we needed. The FDR Archives staff—Kirsten Strigel Carter, Virginia Lewick, Patrick Fahy, Christian Belena, and audio visual specialist Matthew Hanson—could not have been more helpful.

Clifford Laube, the public programs specialist, was a great help as well. And the tour from Scott Rector with the National Park Service really gave us an inside look at how FDR lived on the property growing up and until his death. We also returned to the Eisenhower Library for research into the relationship between FDR and General Eisenhower.

Special thanks to Peter Hubbard, our fabulous editor at William Morrow, for the adult edition. Peter has a keen eye for making something "sing" a little better and all of his edits have made the book that much stronger. Peter and his team really boosted the book from the start.

For the Young Readers' Edition, many thanks to the writer Winifred Conkling, who adapted the text, and to our editor, Alexandra Cooper, for making this a book young people can enjoy and learn from.

As always, thank you to my manager, Larry Kramer, and book agent, Claudia Cross, with Folio Literary Group, for their encouragement and guidance through all three books.

Thank you to my employer, Fox News, for allowing me the time to not only work on the book, but to promote it during a busy news year (all years are busy now, it seems). And for putting together a one-hour documentary around this book, as they did for the other two.

And a very special thank-you to my family—my beautiful wife, Amy, and my two sons, Paul and Daniel. Travel, late nights, and another book tour was not a great thing to look forward to for a family pulled in a lot of different directions . . . but Amy, my rock, held it all together at home and supported me one hundred percent.

Finally, thank you to President Franklin Delano Roosevelt—FDR. His fight to bounce back after being stricken with polio likely made him the president he eventually became. The decisions he made and the relationships he cultivated changed the world, and it's my honor to be able to tell that story.

— GLOSSARY —

ALLIED POWERS: The countries that banded together to fight the Axis Powers during World War II; they included the United States, Great Britain, the Soviet Union, France, Australia, and Belgium.

AXIS POWERS: The countries that banded together to fight the Allies during World War II; they included Germany, Italy, and Japan.

BOLSHEVIK REVOLUTION: Led by Vladimir Lenin and revolutionaries known as Bolsheviks, peasants and working-class Russians revolted against the government of Tsar Nicholas II in 1917.

COLD WAR: The period from 1947 to 1991 when the relationship between the United States and the Soviet Union was characterized by the threat of nuclear war

D-DAY: June 6, 1944, the date of the Allied invasion of Normandy in Operation Overlord

GREAT DEPRESSION: The economic downturn that followed the stock market crash of October 1929 and lasted from 1929 to 1939

LEND-LEASE: A government program to provide Allied countries with military support during World War II, as a way of getting around the country's policy of neutrality

NEW DEAL: A series of programs and projects started during the Great Depression to provide jobs for the unemployed and relief to needy Americans

OPERATION OVERLORD: The code name for the Battle of Normandy, launched on June 6, 1944

POLIO (POLIOMYELITIS): A viral infection that can invade the brain and spinal cord, resulting in paralysis or death

TAMMANY HALL: The name of the Democratic political machine that dominated New York City politics from 1854 to 1934

VICHY FRENCH: The name for the part of France that cooperated with the Nazis during World War II

— SOURCE NOTES —

PROLOGUE: THE "BIG THREE" DINNER PARTY

xvi *"the greatest concentration . . ."*: David L. Roll, *The Hopkins Touch: Harry Hopkins and the Forging of the Alliance to Defeat Hitler* (Oxford, UK: Oxford University Press, 2013).

CHAPTER 1: TO WHOM MUCH IS GIVEN

2 *"Just as the irons . . ."*: (George Will) Ken Burns, *The Roosevelts: An Intimate History*. PBS, 2014.

4 *"I do not believe I have ever seen . . ."*: Sara Delano Roosevelt, as told by Mrs. James Roosevelt to Isabel Leighton and Gabrielle Forbush, *My Boy Franklin* (New York: R. Long & R.R. Smith, 1933).

4 *"Mummie, if I didn't give the orders . . ."*: Ibid.

5 *"The fact is—from my remembrance— . . ."*: Letter from Charles R. Nutter, January 22, 1944. Franklin D. Roosevelt Library correspondence files, archives.

6 *"I am too distressed . . ."*: Franklin D. Roosevelt, letter from Cambridge, "Dearest Mama & Papa," December 3, 1900, in Franklin D. Roosevelt, *F.D.R.: His Personal Letters, Early Years*, edited by

Elliott Roosevelt (New York: Duell, Sloan and Pearce, 1947).

10 *"It probably surprised me only . . ."*: Sara Delano Roosevelt, *My Boy Franklin.*

11 *"We are greatly rejoiced . . ."*: Blanche Wiesen Cook, *Eleanor Roosevelt, Vol. 1: The Early Years, 1884–1933* (New York: Penguin, 1993).

12 *"My father always has to be the bride . . ."*: Burns, *The Roosevelts.*

CHAPTER 2: INTO THE ARENA

14 *"The credit belongs to the man . . ."*: Theodore Roosevelt, "Citizenship in a Republic." Paris, France, April 23, 1910.

14 *"I accept this nomination . . ."*: Franklin D. Roosevelt speech accepting nomination to the state senate, October 6, 1910. Master Speech File, Box 1, FDR Library and Museum.

15 *"What the voters have got to do . . ."*: Roosevelt campaign speech, November 5, 1910. Master Speech File, Box 1, FDR Library and Museum.

15–16 *"I wanted to be independent . . ."*: Eleanor Roosevelt, *The Autobiography of Eleanor Roosevelt* (New York: Harper & Bros., 1961).

16 *"I was so impressed . . ."*: Lela Mae Stiles, *The Man Behind Roosevelt: The Story of Louis McHenry Howe.* (Cleveland: The World Publishing Co., 1954).

17 *"I realized that if . . .":* Eleanor Roosevelt, *Autobiography.*

18 *"I'm as strong as a bull moose":* Letter to Republican manager Mark Hanna in 1900, believed to be Theodore Roosevelt's first use of "bull moose." FDR Presidential Library.

18 *"Friends, I shall ask you . . .":* Patricia O'Toole. "The Speech That Saved Teddy Roosevelt's Life," *Smithsonian Magazine,* November 2012.

19 *"Would you like to come . . .":* James Tertius de Kay, *Roosevelt's Navy: The Education of a Warrior President, 1882–1920* (New York: Pegasus Books, 2013).

19 *"I was very pleased . . .":* Meredith Hindley, "The Roosevelt Bond," *Humanities* 35, no. 5, September–October 2014.

20 *"In half an hour . . .":* James Roosevelt, *Affectionately, F.D.R.: A Son's Story of a Lonely Man* (New York: Harcourt, Brace & Company, 1959).

21 *"The United States must be neutral . . .":* Woodrow Wilson message to Congress on neutrality, August 19, 1914.

22 *"He kept us out of war":* Erick Trickey, "Why Teddy Roosevelt Tried to Bully His Way Onto the World War I Battlefield," *Smithsonian Magazine,* April 10, 2017.

22 *"For ten years I was always . . .":* Eleanor Roosevelt, *Autobiography.*

23 *"Lieutenant Roosevelt . . .":* Eric Durr, "Presidential Son Quentin Roosevelt Was a Famous World War I Casualty," New York National Guard, July 2, 2018.

23 *"I have seen war . . .":* Roosevelt speech in Chautauqua, NY, August 14, 1936. Master Speech File, No. 889. FDR Library and Museum.

26 *"America first":* John A. Morello, *Selling the President 1920: Albert D. Lasker, Advertising, and the Election of Warren G. Harding* (Westport, CT: Praeger Publishers, 2001).

CHAPTER 3: POLIO

27 *"the glow I'd expected . . .":* Jean Edward Smith, *FDR* (New York: Random House, 2007).

29 *"Pa read me . . .":* James Roosevelt, *Affectionately, F.D.R.*

29 *"This is my job . . .":* Ibid.

30 *"The day of the timid . . .":* Ibid.

30 *"I hoped he would devote himself . . .":* Sara Delano Roosevelt, *My Boy Franklin.*

32 *"He steadfastly refused to concede . . .":* Ibid.

33 *"Do you really believe that Franklin . . .":* Smith, *FDR.*

34 *"The governor does not . . .":* Christopher Clausen, "The President and the Wheelchair" *The Wilson Quarterly,* vol. 29, no. 3, Summer 2005.

36 *"Tell me, what would you recommend . . ."*: Samuel Rosenman, *Working with Roosevelt* (New York: Harper & Brothers, 1952).

36 *"I am very mindful . . ."*: Ibid.

38 *"Our government is not the master . . ."*: Roosevelt address to a special session of the New York State legislature, August 28, 1931.

38 *"No one is actually starving . . ."*: Brian Farmer, *American Conservatism: History, Theory and Practice* (Newcastle upon Tyne, UK: Cambridge Scholars Publishing, 2008).

CHAPTER 4: IN THE FOOTSTEPS OF COUSIN TEDDY

40 *"My little man . . ."*: William E. Leuchtenburg, *The American President: From Teddy Roosevelt to Bill Clinton* (New York: Oxford University Press, 2015).

42 *"These unhappy times . . ."*: Roosevelt radio address, April 7, 1932. Master Speech File, No. 469. FDR Library and Museum.

42 *"I am deeply grateful . . ."*: Herbert Hoover, *The Memoirs of Herbert Hoover: The Great Depression, 1929–1941* (New York: Macmillan, 1952).

43 *"I pledge you, I pledge myself . . ."*: Rosenman, *Working with Roosevelt*.

44 *"You know I can't deliver . . ."*: Ibid.

44 *"Out of every crisis . . ."*: Roosevelt speech accepting

the Democratic nomination for president, July 2, 1932. Master Speech File, No. 483. FDR Library and Museum.

47 *"would make up for the blow . . ."*: Eleanor Roosevelt, *Autobiography.*

48 *"You know, Jimmy, all my life . . ."*: James Roosevelt, *Affectionately, F.D.R.*

50 *"Like hell I will . . ."*: Jonathan Alter, *The Defining Moment: FDR's Hundred Days and the Triumph of Hope* (New York: Simon & Schuster, 2006).

CHAPTER 5: PRESIDENT ROOSEVELT

54 *"This is your speech now . . ."*: Robert Schlesinger, *White House Ghosts: Presidents and Their Speechwriters* (New York: Simon & Schuster, 2008).

54 *"Some historians accept . . ."*: Raymond Moley, *The First New Deal* (New York: Harcourt, Brace & World, 1966).

55 *"I am certain that my fellow . . ."*: Roosevelt's first inaugural address, March 4, 1933. FDR Speech File. FDR Library and Museum.

56 *"In preparing a speech . . ."*: Roosevelt papers, FDR Library and Museum.

57 *"Mr. President, as you know . . ."*: James Roosevelt, *Affectionately, F.D.R.*

59 *"The people of the United States . . ."*: Roosevelt's first inaugural address, March 4, 1933. FDR Speech

File. FDR Library and Museum.

59 *"Democracy is not a kind employer . . ."*: Hoover, *Memoirs*.

CHAPTER 6: GOVERNING IN CRISIS

62 *"I am told that what . . ."*: Roosevelt Presidential Press Conference, March 8, 1933.

64 *"Because of undermined . . ."*: Roosevelt's speech on the banking crisis, March 12, 1933. Master Speech File, No. 616-1. FDR Library and Museum.

66 *"I have never told you . . ."*: Carl Sferrazza Anthony, *America's First Families: An Inside View of 200 Years of Private Life in the White House* (New York: Lisa Drew/Simon & Schuster, 2000).

70 *"obligated to promote the victory . . ."*: Adolf Hitler, *Mein Kampf* (Munich: Franz Eher Nachfolger, 1925).

CHAPTER 7: FRANKLIN AND WINSTON

74 *"Far away, happily protected . . ."*: Churchill's radio address, October 16, 1938.

77 *"the new Howe"*: Rosenman, *Working with Roosevelt*.

77 *"I think it would be . . ."*: Roosevelt letter to King George VI, September 17, 1938.

80 *"When peace has been broken . . ."*: Roosevelt's fireside chat, "War in Europe," September 3, 1939. Master Speech File, No. 1240.

80 *"Our bond with Europe . . ."*: Charles Lindbergh's

speech, broadcast on Mutual Radio Network, October 1939.

81 *"I am absolutely convinced . . .":* Morgenthau Diaries, FDR Library.

83 *"As you are no doubt aware . . .":* Warren F. Kimball (ed.), *Churchill & Roosevelt: The Complete Correspondence* (Princeton: Princeton University Press, 1987).

84 *"Washington wouldn't . . .":* John W. Jeffries, *A Third Term for FDR: The Election of 1940* (Lawrence, KS: University Press of Kansas, 2017).

84 *"We want Roosevelt!":* James A. Farley, *Behind the Ballots: The Personal History of a Politician* (New York: Harcourt, Brace & Company, 1938).

86 *"We must look forward . . .":* Rosenman, *Working with Roosevelt.*

87 *"sacred fire of liberty . . .":* Roosevelt's third inaugural address, January 20, 1941. (Reading copy.) FDR Library and Museum.

CHAPTER 8: THE RISE OF THE ALLIES

89 *"Put your confidence in us . . .":* Winston Churchill's radio broadcast, February 9, 1941.

89 *"Suppose my neighbor's home . . .":* Roosevelt Presidential Press Conference, December 17, 1940.

90 *"We have only to kick . . .":* Drew Middleton, "Hitler's Russian Blunder." *New York Times,* June 21, 1981.

90 *"Then, what are we supposed . . .":* Sergei Khrushchev

(ed.), *Memoirs of Nikita Khrushchev, Vol. 1: Commissar 1918–1945* (University Park, PA: Pennsylvania State University Press, 2005).

91 *"No one has been a more consistent . . .":* Winston S. Churchill, *Memoirs of the Second World War* (New York: Houghton Mifflin Company, 1959).

93 *"I address myself . . .":* Roosevelt's message to Emperor Hirohito, December 6, 1941.

CHAPTER 9: THE COMMON CAUSE

95 *"At 7:55 a.m. . . .":* Richard L. Strout, "War Comes to Washington on a Sunday Afternoon," *Christian Science Monitor,* August 22, 1990.

96 *"All hands man . . .":* K. D. Richardson, *Reflections of Pearl Harbor: An Oral History of December 7, 1941* (Westport, CT: Praeger, 2005).

97 *"Yesterday, December 7 . . .":* Franklin D. Roosevelt, "Address to Congress—Declaring War on Japan," December 8, 1941, Master Speech File, no. 1400, Franklin D. Roosevelt Presidential Library and Museum, Hyde Park, NY.

99 *"I have a toast to offer . . .":* Eleanor Roosevelt, "My Day," December 24, 1941. https://www2.gwu.edu/~erpapers/myday/browsebyyear.cfm

100 *"Don't you think so . . .":* Jack Uldrich, *Soldier, Statesman, Peacemaker: Leadership Lessons from George C. Marshall* (New York: AMACOM, 2005).

102 *"I am going to ask . . .":* Rosenman, *Working with Roosevelt.*

104 *"The Secret Service men . . .":* Eleanor Roosevelt, *Autobiography.*

106 *"What can we do to help?"* Churchill, *Memoirs of the Second World War.*

107 *"You may be the man . . .":* Dwight D. Eisenhower, *At Ease: Stories I Tell to Friends* (New York: Doubleday, 1967).

107 *"I will clamp down . . .":* Dwight D. Eisenhower, *Crusade in Europe* (New York: Doubleday, 1948).

108 *"You must not be so afraid . . .":* W. Averell Harriman and Elie Abel, *Special Envoy to Churchill and Stalin, 1941–1946* (New York: Random House, 1975).

108 *"May God help . . .":* Churchill, *Memoirs of the Second World War.*

109 *"This is my Shangri-La!"* Rear Admiral Michael Giorgione, *Inside Camp David: The Private World of the Presidential Retreat* (New York: Little, Brown and Company, 2018).

110 *"We were gambling . . .":* Eisenhower, *Crusade in Europe.*

112 *"Now this is not the end . . .":* Churchill's speech at the Mansion House in London, November 10, 1942.

113 *"Peace can come to the world . . .":* Office of the Historian, Foreign Relations of the United States (FRUS), the Casablanca Conference, January 14–24, 1943.

114 *"We had so much trouble . . .":* Robert E. Sherwood, *Roosevelt and Hopkins: An Intimate History* (New York: Harper & Brothers, 1948).

115 *"He forgot about winter":* Churchill's radio broadcast, May 10, 1942.

CHAPTER 10: THE ROAD TO TEHRAN

120 *"In the absence of a second front . . .":* Stalin's speech, February 22, 1943.

120 *"I know you will not mind . . .":* Kimball (ed.), *Churchill & Roosevelt: The Complete Correspondence.*

121 *"One must not forget . . .":* Susan Butler (ed.), *My Dear Mr. Stalin: The Complete Correspondence of Franklin D. Roosevelt and Joseph V. Stalin* (New Haven: Yale University Press, 2005).

123–24 *"I do not have any objections . . .":* William Harrison Standley, *Admiral Ambassador to Russia* (New York: Regnery, 1955).

124 *"Unfortunately, not one . . .":* Butler, *My Dear Mr. Stalin.*

124 *"It would be regarded . . .":* Ibid.

124 *"I have decided . . .":* Ibid.

125 *"Torpedo defense!"* President's Daily Log, Office of the Historian, Foreign Relations of the United States (FRUS): Diplomatic Papers, the Conferences at Cairo and Tehran, 1943.

125 *"Take me over to the . . .":* William M. Rigdon, *White*

House Sailor (New York: Doubleday, 1962).

126 *"And of course . . ."*: Eleanor Roosevelt, *Autobiography*.

CHAPTER 11: YOUR HOUSE IS MY HOUSE

137 *"Everywhere you went . . ."*: Michael F. Reilly, as told to William J. Slocum, *Reilly of the White House: Behind the Scenes with FDR* (New York: Simon & Schuster, 1947).

139 *"What'd you talk about?"* Elliott Roosevelt, *As He Saw It: The Story of the World Conferences of F.D.R.* (New York: Duell, Sloan and Pearce, 1946).

139 *"new members of the family circle"*: A. H. Birse, *Memoirs of an Interpreter* (New York: Coward-McCann, Inc., 1967).

140 *"was the greatest concentration . . ."*: Roll, *The Hopkins Touch*.

141 *"There I sat . . ."*: Ed Cray, *General of the Army: George C. Marshall, Soldier and Statesman* (New York: Norton, 1990).

141 *"bandit leader"*: William D. Leahy, *I Was There: The Personal Story of the Chief of Staff to Presidents Roosevelt and Truman Based on His Notes and Diaries Made at the Time* (New York: Whittlesey House, 1950).

143 *"Let us first consider . . ."*: Churchill, *Memoirs of the Second World War*.

143 *"Nothing is final . . ."*: Ibid.

CHAPTER 12: CLASH OF TITANS

146 *"It's bizarre"*: Sergo Beria, *Beria, My Father: Inside Stalin's Kremlin* (London: Duckworth Publishing, 2001).

147 *"I have been commanded . . ."*: FRUS: Diplomatic Papers, the Conferences at Cairo and Tehran, 1943.

148 *"Who will command Overlord?"*: Ibid.

148 *"Who bears the moral . . ."*: Ibid.

148 *"We know the men . . ."*: Keith Eubank, *Summit at Teheran* (New York: William Morrow and Company, Inc., 1985).

149 *"Do the prime minister . . ."*: Kenneth W. Thompson, *Winston Churchill's World View, Statesmanship and Power* (Baton Rouge, LA: LSU Press, 1987).

149 *"Provided the conditions . . ."*: Ibid.

150 *"Why do that?"*: Leahy, *I Was There*.

150 *"Our chiefs of staff . . ."*: Elliott Roosevelt, *As He Saw It*.

151 *"There is no need to speak . . ."*: Ibid.

CHAPTER 13: LIKE A RAINBOW

154 *"Truth deserves a bodyguard . . ."*: FRUS: Diplomatic Paper, the Conferences at Cairo and Tehran, 1943.

155 *"a trifle pinker"*: Ibid.

155 *"This is a sign . . ."*: Ibid.

155 *"a symbol of good fortune"*: Ibid.

155 *"We have proven here . . ."*: Ibid.

156 *"Winston, I hope you won't be sore . . ."*: "Teasing Churchill at Tehran." The Churchill Project, July 1, 2016.

156 *"He would have thought . . ."*: Ibid.

160 *"sounds like generalities . . ."*: Charles E. Bohlen, *Witness to History, 1929–1969* (New York: W. W. Norton, 1973).

160 *"Well, Ike, you . . ."*: Eisenhower, *Crusade in Europe*.

161 *"I feel I could not sleep . . ."*: Roll, *The Hopkins Touch*.

161 *"Mr. President, I realize . . ."*: Eisenhower, *Crusade in Europe*.

161 *"I do not remember the president . . ."*: Rosenman, *Working with Roosevelt*.

CHAPTER 14: AT LAST, OVERLORD

165 *"Every obstacle must . . ."*: Eisenhower, *Crusade in Europe*.

166 *"For the sort of . . ."*: Ibid.

167 *"Nice chap. No soldier"*: Nate Rawlings, "Top 10 Across-the-Pond Duos: Montgomery and Eisenhower," *Time*, June 20, 2010.

167 *"General Montgomery has no superior . . ."*: Eisenhower, *Crusade in Europe*.

168 *"When I think of the beaches . . ."*: Eisenhower, *At Ease*.

168 *"General, if by the coming winter . . ."*: Ibid.

169 *"futile slaughter"*: Eisenhower, *Crusade in Europe*.

169 *"I went to my tent alone . . ."*: Eisenhower, *Crusade in Europe*.

170 *"Okay, we'll go"*: There are different versions of Eisenhower's actual words. According to Timothy Rives, acting director of the Dwight D. Eisenhower Presidential Library, Ike's chief of staff, Lieutenant General Bedell Smith, recalled, "Well, we'll go." Intelligence officer Major General Kenneth Strong recalled, "Okay, boys, we will go." Eisenhower himself recalled, "Okay, we'll go" in an interview with Walter Cronkite.

170 *"Our landings in the Cherbourg-Havre . . ."*: Ibid.

171 *"There's not going to be . . ."*: David Irving, *The Trail of the Fox* (New York: Dutton, 1977).

172 *"We'll start the war . . ."*: Jesse Greenspan, "Landing at Normandy: The 5 Beaches of D-Day," History .com, August 30, 2018.

174 *"D-day has come"*: Robert Strunsky and Paul M. Hollister, *From D-Day Through Victory in Europe: The Eyewitness Story as Told by War Correspondents on the Air* (New York: Columbia Broadcasting System, 1945).

174 *"The tide has turned . . ."*: Ibid.

174 *"People of Western Europe . . ."*: Ibid.

174 *"Very heavy firing . . ."*: Ibid.

175 *"Almighty God: Our sons . . ."*: Roosevelt's D-Day Prayer. Master Speech File, No. 1519, June 6, 1944.

175 *"Everything has started well . . ."*: Churchill, *Memoirs of the Second World War.*

176 *"serious difficulty"*: Churchill, *Memoirs of the Second World War.*

176 *"History will record . . ."*: Ibid.

176 *"From the start of Overlord . . ."*: Eisenhower, *At Ease.*

CHAPTER 15: FDR'S FINAL ACT

177 *"I found the Boss . . ."*: Grace Tully, *F.D.R. My Boss* (Chicago: Peoples Book Club, 1949).

179 *"Mr. Roosevelt did not want . . ."*: A. Merriman Smith, *Thank You, Mr. President: A White House Notebook* (New York: Harper & Brothers, 1946).

180 *"The man had one . . ."*: David M. Jordan, *FDR, Dewey, and the Election of 1944* (Bloomington: Indiana University Press, 2011).

181 *"The Vice President simply . . ."*: David McCullough, *Truman* (New York: Simon & Schuster, 1992).

181 *"1600 Pennsylvania . . ."*: Ibid.

182 *"Anyone with a grain . . ."*: James A. Farley, *Jim Farley's Story: The Roosevelt Years* (New York: Whittlesey House, 1948).

183 *"Dog catchers have . . ."*: Reilly, *Reilly of the White House.*

183 *"The first twelve years . . ."*: Roosevelt, Presidential Press Conference, January 19, 1945.

183 *"his face looked thin . . ."*: Frances Perkins, *The Roosevelt I Knew* (New York: Viking, 1946).

184 *"I am firmly convinced . . ."*: Bohlen, *Witness to History.*

185 *"We specifically desired . . ."*: Edward R. Stettinius, *Roosevelt and the Russians: The Yalta Conference* (New York: Doubleday, 1950).

186 *"If we had spent ten years . . ."*: Office of the Historian, Foreign Relations of the United States (FRUS), Diplomatic Papers, the Conferences at Malta and Yalta.

186 *"You can't . . ."*: Reilly, *Reilly of the White House.*

186 *"I saw the kind of reckless . . ."*: Roosevelt's speech to Congress on the Yalta Conference, March 1, 1945. Master Speech File, No. 1572, A, B. FDR Library and Museum.

187 *"peace should be written . . ."*: Office of the Historian, Foreign Relations of the United States (FRUS), Diplomatic Papers, the Conferences at Malta and Yalta.

188 *"If I could see . . ."*: James F. Byrnes, *Speaking Frankly* (New York: Harper & Brothers Publishers, 1947).

189 *"I agree that the French . . ."*: Ibid.

189 *"We were all in difficulties . . ."*: Ibid.

189 *"Britain declared war . . ."*: Ibid.

190 *"For the Russian people . . ."*: Ibid.

190 *"I am called a dictator . . ."*: Ibid.

190 *"How long before elections . . ."*: Ibid.

191 *"I only want to have . . ."*: Harriman and Abel, *Special Envoy.*

193 *"History has recorded . . ."*: Stettinius, *Roosevelt and the Russians.*

193 *"It is the story . . ."*: Lord Moran, *Churchill at War* (New York: Carroll & Graf, 2002).

CHAPTER 16: THE WORLD HE LEFT BEHIND

194 *"Of course, we know . . ."*: Roosevelt's speech to Congress on the Yalta Conference, March 1, 1945. Master Speech File, No. 1572, A, B. FDR Library and Museum.

195 *"I feel that your information . . ."*: Butler (ed.), *My Dear Mr. Stalin.*

196 *"I have never doubted . . ."*: Ibid.

196 *"I have a terrific pain . . ."*: Geoffrey C. Ward, ed., *Closest Companion: The Unknown Story of the Intimate Friendship Between Franklin Roosevelt and Margaret Suckley* (New York: Houghton Mifflin, 1995).

197 *"DARLINGS: PA SLEPT . . ."*: James Roosevelt, *Affectionately, F.D.R.*

200 *"I myself and my wife . . ."*: Lily Rothman, "How the World Learned of Hitler's Death," *Time*, April 30, 2015.

200 *"When the signing . . .":* Eisenhower, *At Ease.*

200 *"a new weapon . . .":* McCullough, *Truman.*

201 *"The enemy has begun . . .":* Emperor Hirohito Accepting the Potsdam Declaration (radio address), August 14, 1945.

203 *"We are still in the generality . . .":* Roosevelt, Presidential Press Conference, December 28, 1943.

203 *"Roosevelt knew how to conceal . . .":* V. M. Molotov and Felix Chuev, *Molotov Remembers: Inside Kremlin Politics* (trans.) (Chicago: Ivan R. Dee, 1993).

204 *"A freely elected . . .":* Philip Edward Mosely, *Face to Face with Russia.* Foreign Policy Association Headline Series, 1948.

206 *"During the dark days . . .":* Ronald Reagan, speech to the House of Commons, June 8, 1982.

— INDEX —

*Page numbers in italics refer to
photographs.*

affairs, 24
Agricultural Adjustment Act, 67
Allied Powers, 102, 211
    in Italy, 122–23
    victories of, 185
armistice agreements, 122–23
arm strength, 31–33
assassination attempt, 1933, xv–
    xvi, 49
Atlantic Charter, 92
atom bomb, 182
    attacks with, 201
    Truman, Harry S., on, 201
attrition, 140
Axis Powers, 211
    formalizing, 85

bank holiday, 64
Bataan, 101
Berlin, 199–200
Bethesda Naval Hospital, 178
the Big Three allies, xiv, xvi,

xviii, 124, 156, 190
    on Japan, 200–201
    meeting of, 120, 139–40
    tensions among, 195
Black Sea, xvii, 186–87
Bolshevik Revolution, 104, 211
Bonus Army, 45–46
Brain Trust, 41
Braun, Eva, 200
bronchial infection, 177–78
Buckingham Palace, 85
"The Building of the Ship"
    (Longfellow), 88–89
Bull Moose Party, 18

Camp David, 109
Campobello, 5–7, 27
capitalism, 79
    Stalin on, 205
Casablanca, 112, 113
Catoctin Mountains, 109
CCC. *See* Civilian Conservation
    Corps
cerebral hemorrhage, 196–97
Cermak, Anton, 49

Cherbourg-Havre, 170–71
childhood, 2–3
China, 125
  Stalin on, 147
Churchill, Winston, xiv, *132*
  birthday dinner of, 155
  on Communism, 91, 155
  Eisenhower meeting with, 168
  FDR and, xi, 72–73, 83, 88–89, 106, 121, 126, 135, 145–46, 156–57, 184
  flaws of, 74
  on France, 112–13, 140–41, 188–89
  on Germany, 188
  on Hitler, 71, 74
  on Japan, 99
  on Mediterranean, 149
  in Moscow, 107–8, 184
  on Munich Pact, 72–73
  on North Africa, 112
  on Operation Overlord, 149–50, 175–76
  on Poland, 189–90
  postwar needs of, 187–88
  on Rome, 141
  Stalin and, 108, 138, 147, 151, 184–85
  at Tehran Conference, xvi–xvii, 140–41
  USS *Augusta* meeting with FDR, 91–92

citizenship
  of Japanese Americans, 101
  Roosevelt, Teddy, on, 13–14
Civilian Conservation Corps (CCC), 65
Civil Works Administration (CWA), 65
Cleveland, Grover, 40
Cold War, 211
  aftermath of, 204
  beginning of, 206
Common Cause, 99, 151
Communism, 46
  Churchill on, 91, 155
  Stalin and, 123
  Standley on, 123
concentration camps, 76
Cook, Nancy, 34
Cox, James M., 25
Crimea, 185
Crimson (newspaper), 7
cross-Channel invasion, 140
cross-examination, 62
CWA. *See* Civil Works Administration
Czechoslovakia, 72, 75

Daladier, Édouard, 72
Daniels, Josephus, 18–19
Darlan, Jean-François, 111
D-Day, 211
  airborne divisions in, 166, 171

anniversary of, ix
Eisenhower in, *133*, 166–67
Eisenhower's Order of the
    Day, 174
eve of, *133*
Germany on, 171
ground forces on, 166–67
planning for, 165
success of, 176
timing of, 167
troops in, 167–68
death, 196–97
Declaration of the Three
    Powers, 159–60
de Gaulle, Charles, 110–11
    meeting with, 113
Delano, Warren, 3
Democracy, 59
Democratic National
    Convention, 25, *128*, 180
    1924, 32–33
Democrats, 6, 16
    in 1934 midterm elections,
        66
Department of Veterans Affairs,
    ix
Dewey, Thomas, 180
Dickerman, Marion, 34
Douglas, William O., 180
Dzhugashvili, Iosif
    Vissarionovich. *See* Stalin,
    Joseph

Early, Stephen, 61
Eastern Europe, Stalin on, 184–
    85, 204
editing, 56
education
    of FDR, 3–4
    of Roosevelt, Eleanor, 9–10
Eisenhower, Dwight D., x,
    99–100, 107, 110, 199
    Berlin, 199
    Churchill meeting with, 168
    in D-Day, *133*, 166–67
    on failure, 170–71
    FDR and, 111–12, 160–61
    misinformation campaign
        of, 122
    on Montgomery, 167
    on Operation Overlord,
        160–61
    Order of the Day, 174
    on planning, 165
    on troops, 167
    on World War II, 176
Eisenhower Library, xi
elitism, 16–17
Elizabeth (Queen), 77–78
Emergency Banking Relief Act,
    64
emergency powers, Hitler
    granted, 70–71
English Channel, xviii

Fairbanks, Alaska, 120–21

famine, 79
Farley, James A., 41, 43
fatherhood, 19–20
FDR. *See* Roosevelt, Franklin Delano
fear, 54–55
Federal Emergency Relief Act (FERA), 64–65
Ferdinand, Franz, 20
fireside chats, 63–64
Four Freedoms speech, 86
Four Policemen, Stalin on, 147
France, xviii, 23
    Churchill on, 112–13, 140–41, 188–89
    leadership of, 112–13
    Stalin on, 140–41
    surrender of, to Germany, 110–11
Franklin D. Roosevelt Presidential Library and Museum, x
free elections, 204–6
Free French (resistance government), 110, 113
funeral, 198–99

Garner, John Nance, 44, 180
George VI (King), 77–78, 147, 168–69
Georgia, 30–31, 34
Georgia Warm Springs Foundation for Infantile Paralysis, 34
German Workers' Party, 69
Germany, 21–22
    Churchill on, 188
    on D-Day, 171
    dividing, 158
    FDR and, 150, 158
    France surrendering to, 110–11
    nonaggression pact with Soviet Union, 78–79, 89–90
    Stalin on, 143–44, 159, 188, 204–5
    United States and, 195
    in World War II, 85
Gestapo, 71
GI Bill, 206
Giraud, Henri, 112–13
Glass-Steagall Act, 64–65
Gold Beach, 172–73
golf, 5–6
Gorbachev, Mikhail, xi
governor elections, 1928, 35
Grant, Ulysses S., 114
Great Depression, 2, 104, 109, 211
    beginning of, 36–37
    Hoover on, 42
    New Deal and, 75
    taxes in, 37–38
    unemployment in, 37
Greatest Generation, x

Great Purge, 79

Groton Missionary Society, 5

Groton School, 29

   graduation from, 5–6

"Hail to the Chief," 198–99

Hall, Anna Rebecca, 9

Harding, Warren, 25–26

Harvard College, 6

Harvard Law School, 2–3

health, declining, 178, 182–83

Hearst, William Randolph, 44

Hindenburg, Paul von, 70

Hirohito (Emperor), 93–94,
   201–2

Hiroshima, Japan, 201

Hitler, Adolf, xiii, 122, *130*, 176

   Churchill on, 71, 74

   emergency powers granted
      to, 70–71

   FDR and, 75

   imprisonment of, 70

   Jewish people treated by,
      75–76

   Mein Kampf, 70

   negotiation with, 114

   nonaggression pact broken
      by, 89–90

   Poland invaded by, 80

   rise of, 68–69

   Soviet Union attacked by,
      89–90, 204

   Stalin on, 204–5

   suicide of, 200

Hong Kong, 151

Hoover, Herbert, 35, 36–37

   criticizing, 42

   FDR and, 37–38, 50, 57–58

   on Great Depression, 42

   in 1932 elections, 42–43

Hoover, Lou, 58

Hopkins, Harry, xix, 77, 91

Howe, Louis McHenry, 16–17,
   43, 44, 60

   assistance from, 29–30

   death of, 67

Hyde Park, 54

inauguration

   in 1945, 183

   in 1941, 86–89

   in 1937, 67–68

   in 1933, 57–60

internment camps, in United
   States, 101

Iran, *134*, 136

   shah of, 153

isolationism, 80–81

Italy

   Allied Powers in, 122–23

   in World War II, 83–85

Japan

   attrition in war with, 140

   the Big Three on, 200–201

Japan (*continued*)
Churchill on, 99
declaration of war against, 98
defeats of, 185
FDR and, 92–93
Soviet Union and, 125–26,
192
Stalin on, 187–88
United States at war with,
140
in World War II, 85, 96,
105–6
Japanese Americans
citizenship of, 101
during World War II, 101
Jefferson, Thomas, 181–82
Jewish people, 69
FDR and, 76–77
Hitler's treatment of, 75–76
Jordan, David M., 180

Kai-shek, Chiang, 125
Kennedy, Joseph, 77
Khrushchev, Nikita, 90
Knox, Franklin, 82
Kristallnacht, 76
Kurusu, Saburo, 93

leadership
FDR and, 2, 4
of France, 112–13
League of Nations, 25

Leahy, William, 108–9
Lend-Lease Act, 89, 96–97, 120,
211–12
liberty, 87
Libya, 106
Lincoln Study, 59
Lindbergh, Charles, 77
Nazism of, 80–81
Livadia Palace, 187
Lowell, Abbott Lawrence, 7
Lublin, 189

MacArthur, Douglas, 46
Madison, James, 181–82
Malta, 185
Marshall, George C., 82, 87,
100, 107, 161
Marx, Karl, 79
McKinley, William, 6
the Mediterranean, 141
Churchill on, 149
Mein Kampf (Hitler), 70
Mercer, Lucy, 19, 21, 195
affair with FDR, 24
renewed relationship with
FDR, 178–79, 197–98
Roosevelt, Eleanor, and, 197
military diplomacy, 154
military exclusion zones, 101
Moley, Raymond, 41, 43, 53, 67
Molotov, Vyacheslav, 104
FDR and, 104–5
Montgomery, Bernard Law,

Eisenhower on, 167
Moscow, 91
  Churchill in, 107–8, 184
Munich Pact, 75
  Churchill on, 72–73
Murrow, Edward R., 174
Mussolini, Benito, 72
  regime of, ended, 122

Nagasaki, Japan, 201
National Industrial Recovery
  Act, 67
nationalism, 68–69
Navy Department (US), 62
Nazis, xiv, 25, 69–70
  in Kristallnacht, 76
  Lindbergh and, 80–81
  power of, 70–71
Nesbitt, Henrietta, 65
Neutrality Acts, 81
New Deal, 43–45, 212
  beginning of, 64–65
  Great Depression and, 75
  popularity of, 66–67
  Supreme Court on, 67
New York Herald, 16–17
Nicholas (Tsar), 186
Nineteenth Amendment, 25
NKVD (secret police), xvi
Nomura, Kichisaburo, 93
nonaggression pact (Germany
  and Soviet Union), 78–79
  Hitler breaking, 89–90

Normandy, ix, 133
North Africa, 105–6
  Churchill on, 112
nuclear technology, of Soviet
  Union, 202–3, 206

Oahu, 95–96
Omaha Beach, 173, 176
101st Airborne Division, 170
Operation Overlord, ix, 133,
  140, 212. See also D-Day
  Churchill on, 149–50,
    175–76
  commander of, 148, 154
  delaying, 170
  Eisenhower on, 160–61
  FDR and, 148–49, 175
  planning for, 165
  Stalin on, 148, 176
Operation Torch, 110–11
Order of the Day, Eisenhower,
  174

paratroopers, 171
Parish, Susie, 11
peace, 202
Pearl Harbor, 95–96, 130, 131
  FDR on attack on, 97–98
Perkins, Frances, 48
personality, 1–2
Pisa–Rimini line, 153
Poland, 157–58

Poland (*continued*)

    Churchill on, 189–90

    FDR on, 158

    Hitler's invasion of, 80, *130*

    Soviet Union and, 190–91

    Stalin on, 144, 158

polio, 26–27, 212

    diagnosis with, 28

    recovery from, 30–31

politburo, 195

political campaigns, 83–85, 180–81

Potsdam Conference, 201, 203

presidential elections

    1940, 83–85

    1944, 182–83

    1932, 42–47

    1920, 25–26

press conferences, 61, *129*

public life, *128*

Public Works Administration (PWA), 64–65

Quebec, 123

Rankin, Jeannette, 98

Reagan, Ronald, x, 206

Red Army (Soviet), 136

reformism, 18

Reilly, Mike, 137

Republicans, 6

Reza (Shah), 153

RMS *Lusitania*, 21

Rome, Churchill on importance of, 141

Rommel, Erwin, 171

Roosevelt, Anna (daughter), 15–16, *127*, 197

Roosevelt, Eleanor (wife), *127*, 197

    childhood of, 9

    children of, 12

    education of, 9–10

    marriage to FDR, 10–12

    meeting, 8–9

    Mercer and, 197

    as mother, 19–20

    news conferences of, 63

    pregnancies of, 12, 15–16

    relationship with FDR, 9–10, 12, 24

    Roosevelt, Sara, and, 66

    Secret Service and, 66

    social life of, 34

    in Washington, 19

    on women's rights, 63

Roosevelt, Elliott (son), 9, 15–16, 97, 125, *127*

    FDR and, 139

Roosevelt, Franklin, Jr. (son), 15–16, 97, 125, *127*

Roosevelt, Franklin Delano. *See also specific topics*

    as authority, 35

    campaigns of, 83–85, 180–81

cerebral hemorrhage of, 196–97

as champion of common folk, 1–2

childhood of, 2–3

Churchill and, xi, 72–73, 83, 88–89, 106, 121, 126, 135, 145–46, 156–57, 184

comeback of, *128*

death of, 196–97

education of, 3–4

Eisenhower and, 111–12, 160–61

as father, 19–20

on fear, 54–55

fireside chats of, 63–64

on Germany, 150, 158

on Hitler, 75

Hoover and, 37–38, 50, 57–58

image of, 35

inaugurations, 57–60, 67–68, 86–89, 183

Japan and, 92–93

Jewish people and, 76–77

leadership of, 2, 4

Molotov and, 104–5

on Operation Overlord, 148–49, 175

on Pearl Harbor attack, 97–98

on Poland, 158

political climb of, 26

presidential elections, 25–26, 42–47, 83–85, 182–83

public life of, *128*

Roosevelt, Elliott, and, 139

Rosenman and, 161

on Soviet Union, 91

speeches of, 53–57, 63–64, 86, *128, 129*

Stalin and, xi–xvii, 120–21, 136–38, 184, 195–96, 202–3, 205

as strategist, xviii–xix

study room of, *134*

at Tehran Conference, 140–42, 155–56

Truman, Harry S., on, 182

on United Nations, 146–47

USS Augusta meeting with Churchill, 91–92

wheelchair of, 32–33, *134*

at Yalta Conference, 203

Roosevelt, James (Rosy), 3, 15–16, 29, 48, 57, *127*

in World War II, 97

Roosevelt, John (son), 22, 97, *127*

Roosevelt, Quentin (nephew), 23

Roosevelt, Sara (mother), 1, 7, 11–12, 30

death of, 92

on health, 30

as mother, 3, *127*

Roosevelt, Sara (*continued*)
    Roosevelt, Eleanor, and, 66
Roosevelt, Teddy (cousin), 6, 82
    assassination attempt on, 18
    on citizenship, 13–14
    relationship with, 7–8, 18–19
Roosevelt, Theodore, Jr.
    (nephew), 172
Roosevelt Republicans, 8
Rosenman, Samuel, 35–36, 43,
    55, 77
    FDR and, 161
Russia, xiv
Rutherfurd, Lucy Mercer. *See*
    Mercer, Lucy
Rutherfurd, Winthrop, 178–79

Sainte-Mère-Église, 172
Saint John's Episcopal Church,
    58
Saint Patrick's Day Parade, 11
SEC. *See* Securities and
    Exchange Commission
Secret Service, 136
    Roosevelt, Eleanor, and, 66
Securities and Exchange
    Commission (SEC), 65
self-doubt, 48
senate
    appointments made in, 16
    reelection to, 17–18
    running for, 14–15
Sicily campaign, 122

Singapore, 101, 151
Smith, Al, 32, 34, *128*
Smith, Merriman, 179–80
Social Security Act, 49
    passage of, 67
social security bill, 66–67
Soviet Embassy, xv
Soviet Union
    cooperation with, 203
    FDR and, 91
    Hitler attacking, 89–90
    Japan and, 125–26, 192
    nonaggression pact with
      Germany, 78–79, 89–90
    nuclear technology of, 202–
      3, 206
    Poland and, 190–91
    postwar, 144
    United Kingdom and, 192
    United States and, 151,
      203–4
    victory of, at Stalingrad, 115
    in World War II, 204
special interests, 14–15
speeches, *128*, *129*
    fireside chats, 63–64
    Four Freedoms, 86
    writing, 53–57
sports, 5
Stalin, Joseph, xiv, 79, 102–3,
    132, 143, 195
    ambitions of, 150–51
    on capitalism, 205

on China, 147
Churchill and, 108, 138, 151, 184–85
Communism and, 123
on Eastern Europe, 184–85, 204
FDR and, xi–xvii, 120–21, 136–38, 184, 195–96, 202–3, 205
on Four Policemen, 147
on France, 140–41
on Germany, 143–44, 159, 188, 204–5
on Hitler, 204–5
on Japan, 187–88, 191–92
on Operation Overlord, 148, 176
partnership with, xix
on Poland, 144, 158
postwar needs of, 187–88
Standley and, 103–4, 120, 123
Sword of Stalingrad received by, 147–48
at Tehran Conference, xvi–xvii, 136–40, 193
Truman, Harry S., and, 205
on unconditional surrender, 142
at Yalta Conference, 203
Stalingrad, 90, 112, 147
Soviet victory at, 115
Standley, William

on Communism, 123
Stalin and, 103–4, 120, 123
Stettinius, Edward, 185
Truman, Harry S., and, 203
Stimson, Henry, 82, 101
strategist, xviii–xix
study, *134*
Suckley, Daisy, 195
Sudetenland, 72
Suez Canal, 106
suffrage, 17
Supreme Court
changing, 67–68
on New Deal, 67
Sword of Stalingrad, 147–48

Taft, William Howard, 17–18
Tammany Hall, 15, 212
"Taps," 199
taxes, in Great Depression, 37–38
Tehran Conference, ix, xv, *132*, *134*, 135, 202–3
bugged rooms at, xvi
Churchill at, xvi–xvii, 140–41
extension of, 152
FDR at, 140–42, 155–56
scheduling, 124
Stalin at, xvi–xvii, 136–40, 193
Telegraph Cottage, 166
term limits, 82

Thanksgiving, 125–26
Tobruk, Libya, 106
totalitarianism, 143–44
Tripartite Pact, 85
Truman, Harry S., 180–81, 198
    on atomic bomb, 201
    on FDR, 182
    Stalin and, 205
    Stettinius and, 203
Truman, Margaret, 199
Tully, Grace, 178, 181
Tunisia, 111

Uncle Joe. *See* Stalin, Joseph
unconditional surrender, 114,
    200–201
    Stalin on, 142
United Kingdom
    allies of, 78–79
    Soviet Union and, 192
    United States and, 105–6
    in World War II, 83–84, 85
United Nations
    FDR on, 146–47
    first meeting of, 192
United States, 158
    Germany and, 195
    internment camps in, 101
    neutrality of, 81
    postwar, 205–6
    Soviet Union and, 151, 203–4
    United Kingdom and, 105–6

war with Japan, 140
    in World War II, 96–97
USS *Augusta*, 91–92
USS *Iowa*, 124
USS *Quincy*, 185
USS *Shangri-La*, 109
    Churchill at, 121
Utah Beach, 172

Val-Kill stream, 34
veterans, death rates of, ix
vice presidency, 180–81
Vichy French, 111, 212

Wallace, Henry, 180
Warm Springs, *134*, 195
Washington, George, 82, 87
Washington, Roosevelt,
    Eleanor, in, 19
Watson, Edwin, 82
West Point, x
wheelchair, 32–33, *134*
Will, George, 2
Willkie, Wendell, 84
Wilson, Woodrow, 18, 21, 25
women's rights, Roosevelt,
    Eleanor, on, 63
Works Progress Administration
    (WPA), 109
World War I, 20–21, 45, 80
    controls after, 144
    United States in, 21–22

World War II, ix
  Eisenhower on, 176
  Germany in, 85
  Italy in, 83–85
  Japanese Americans during,
    101
  Japan in, 85, 105–6
  optimism after end of, 205–6
  Roosevelt, James, in, 97
  second front in, 119–20

  Soviet Union in, 204
  United Kingdom in, 83–84,
    85
WPA. *See* Works Progress
  Administration

Yalta Conference, xvii, 186,
  194–95, 202
  FDR at, 203
  Stalin at, 203